So Be Encouraged: Breakfast with Jesus

A Daily Devotional for Men & Women

Laurine Voltaire

WESTBOW
PRESS®
A DIVISION OF THOMAS NELSON
& ZONDERVAN

WestBow Press books may be ordered through booksellers or by contacting:

WestBow Press
A Division of Thomas Nelson & Zondervan
1663 Liberty Drive
Bloomington, IN 47403
www.westbowpress.com
1 (866) 928-1240

Because of the dynamic nature of the Internet, any web addresses or
links contained in this book may have changed since publication and
may no longer be valid. The views expressed in this work are solely those
of the author and do not necessarily reflect the views of the publisher,
and the publisher hereby disclaims any responsibility for them.

Any people depicted in stock imagery provided by Getty Images are
models, and such images are being used for illustrative purposes only.
Certain stock imagery © Getty Images.

ISBN: 978-1-9736-6087-3 (sc)
ISBN: 978-1-9736-6086-6 (hc)
ISBN: 978-1-9736-6088-0 (e)

Library of Congress Control Number: 2019904809

Print information available on the last page.

WestBow Press rev. date: 09/17/2019

Foreword

Since the beginning of the Christian Church, believers have gathered to study the sacred scriptures, break bread together and share in corporate worship. From the Book of Acts to the present day, praying for one another, encouraging one another, and bearing witness to Christ's love, have continued to be hallmarks of the practice of Christianity. Yet, one of the lessons that has not transferred well from the early days is the understanding that our collective gatherings of worship are empowered by our individual time in personal devotion. In essence, we are inspired, encouraged and tremendously blessed corporately when we bring the overflow of our individual praise and adoration from our personal time with Jesus. It is this lesson that makes **_So Be Encouraged: Breakfast with Jesus_** an important devotional. What a privilege to accept the daily invitation to enjoy quality time with Jesus over the most important meal of the day.

Laurine Voltaire is a brilliant exegete with a deep calling to stimulate a renewal of committed, daily, and intimate time with Jesus. Grounded in scripture and anchored with a closing prayer, the devotions in this collection offer an invitation for the Holy Spirit to speak while also availing a powerful dose of inspiration for real people, facing real life, in real time. This book is a collection of healthy recipes full of ample portions of faith, hope, and love offered to inspire daily engagement with our Lord and Savior. Be encouraged and enjoy your standing reservation with Jesus!

Bon Appétit,

Emmett G. Price III
Professor & Dean,
Gordon-Conwell Theological Seminary

Dedication

"Heaven has gained a beautiful Rose named Marie Adolphe"- Laurine Voltaire

My mother was always my biggest cheerleader. Ever since I was a young girl, she always supported my passion to write. When I was a teenager, I would write spoken-words and she would encourage me to read them at church even though I was afraid of speaking in public. My mother was the first person to lend me a listening ear and she always made time to hear, what the Father was downloading into my heart to share with His people. Those times were so precious to me.

When my compilation of poems increased, she encouraged me to write a book. I never did publish that one, *maybe later Mom*, but I know she would be proud of this one. As time went by, in my young adult years, my mother saw that I was constantly writing in my journals, and she said to me about a thousand times, "Lolo, it is time to write your book." I knew that it was God impressing this message on her heart to propel me forward. So now, by God's grace, I can finally say, *"Mom, the book is here and it is all because you never stopped praying for me and believing that greatness was inside of me."*

To you my dearest mother Marie Rose Adolphe do I dedicate this book. Thank you for all the times you have encouraged me, thank you for the times you listened to my heart, and thank you for raising me to love Jesus. Miss you, love you, and see you again.

Contents

PART 1.

Inviting Jesus In:

Let Jesus Become Your Everything

Devotion 1: Meal For Two

"If you have the courage to let Christ into every room of your life, He will come in and redecorate your life, so that it is more beautiful than you have ever imagined possible. But you'll never know until you start opening those doors." – Ray Pritchard

Every day of our lives, we have the privilege to sit down in the presence of royalty, to eat a meal with our beloved Jesus. We have the pleasure to be partakers of His Holy Word, thus carefully listening to everything He has to say to us. While we are spending time with Jesus, His gracious words burn deeply in our hearts. Some of us may think that we are not worthy of this honor (and trust me, we are not), but *Jesus still chooses to have us sit with Him, so that we can get acquainted with His presence, and He can get acquainted with our hearts.* In Revelation 3:20 Jesus invites the church, His people, to dine with Him. Jesus says, "Behold, I stand at the door and knock. If anyone hears My voice and opens the door, I will come in and eat with Him, and we will share a meal together as friends" (Revelation 3:20 NLT). Jesus the victorious Savior, who defeated the devil, death, sin, and the grave all at once, is offering to share a meal with you. A meal that was purchased with a sacrificial love. What an honor!

Jesus is looking for more than just a meet and greet in which both parties briefly introduce themselves and then depart, never to see each other again. Jesus wants to get cozy with you on a nice comfy couch, by a fireplace, where He can get to know you as you get to know Him. Jesus wants to be your friend and He wants to be the type of friend that you enjoy spending time with. That is why He knocks, to get our hearts' attention to focus only on our one true love.

Dining with Jesus is a two-way communion process. While Jesus is eating with us, we are also choosing to reciprocate the gesture by accepting His invitation. Reciprocation is key because no one wants to dine where they are not welcomed. No one wants to come in and sit down when a place has not been freely opened to them. Picture this: A friend invites you to his or her house for the first time. When you get to the front door, you certainly wouldn't just pull out your own keys, and try to open it. That would just be silly. Instead, you ring the doorbell and wait for your friend, in anticipation, that he or she will come and open the door for you. And when your friend finally opens the door, immediately you hear these comforting words, "Come in and make yourself at home." At that very moment, you know for sure, that you have come to a place where you are welcomed. That is what Jesus is waiting for us to do: to invite Him into our hearts so He can make our hearts His home.

For Jesus to make our hearts His home, we are going to have to get rid of everything that does not look like Jesus and everything that has been taking His place as lord in our hearts. This includes all the hidden things: all the evil and wicked habits, addictions, thoughts, and attitudes. Some of you may be thinking, "Oh gosh. If I allow Jesus to come all the way into my heart, He may not want to stay. There is too much going on in here that I do not even want to deal with myself." Do not panic! Jesus would never just barge in and start demanding us to change everything at once. Jesus is a gentleman and He gives us time. He takes the time to show us things about ourselves that, we will eventually agree, needs to change. Jesus is very patient with us. No matter what is hidden in your heart, no matter the sin, the muck or the guck, Jesus has come to wash it clean. Today, He has also come to grant you forgiveness, and give you peace, and He desires to heal all your inner wounds. He thoroughly heals us as He tenderly takes care of us. The process of healing doesn't always feel good, but it is for our good and it feels marvelous once it's done.

Remember that invitation to your friend's house and that warm welcome? Well, you do not really make yourself at home until your friend finds a place for you to sit down, which signifies rest. So be encouraged to make room for Jesus to sit on the throne of your heart today; for He has come to give you rest for a lifetime.

Right now, while you are reading this, Jesus is softly knocking on the door of your heart. Do not be scared to let Jesus come in. Dine with Him, linger in His presence, sit at His feet, and commune with your Savior. Choose to return to your first love. Choose the better thing today, as Mary did in Luke chapter 10:42, which is to wait and rest at the feet of Jesus. I pray that, as you rest at His feet, you will receive your supply and fill from your Savior's hand. For only in Jesus, will you be satiated to your heart's content, filled to the brim, and filled to the overflow.

<u>PRAYER:</u>

"Father, I open the gates of my heart for Jesus to come in. I welcome you, Jesus, to come into my heart today as a friend. I want to become best friends with you, Jesus. I give you your rightful place to sit on the throne of my heart as Lord and King. I humble myself before you, thankful that you have chosen me to be your dining partner. Jesus, may I receive my fill from you today. Everything that you have planned to give me, I gratefully receive it. I receive your love, blessings, peace, inner healing, joy, and your precious divine promises for my life. I want your will to be done. Thank you, Lord. In Jesus' name, I pray, Amen."

<u>Devotion 2: Encourage Yourself</u>

"The Word of God coming out of your mouth is stronger than anything that has ever been said to you." – Joyce Meyers

Sometimes in life, you must be your own cheerleader. You are going to have to purchase your own pair of pompoms, throw your own pep rally, break out your best dance moves and begin to shout with loud praises with a voice of triumph. ***Learn to encourage yourself in the midst of your storm!*** For far too long, you have depended on what everyone else thinks is best, and you have depended on their words to carry you through instead of leaning on God's Word. It is time for you to clothe yourself with His truth. Then, you will know that everything is going to be all right even though your circumstances do not seem like it.

Self-motivation and building yourself up is not prideful. They are about assuring yourself in God's love and in His promises over your life, but with your own mouth. I am all for prophetic words and receiving words of affirmation from loved ones, but I believe there comes a point in time when you have to speak those words back to yourself as a reminder that you are blessed and dearly loved. There will be times when your mother, father, best friends, or mentors will not be around to tell you what you need to do. They will not always be there to pray you through your hardest times. There are times in your life, I believe, God purposely does not allow your friends to pick up the phone in the late-night hours when you are in dire need of some help. In these moments, you are not alone. God is right there beside you. He is testing your heart and encouraging you to exercise the faith He has given you.

It is imperative that you develop a lifestyle of daily recitation and confessions of God's faithful promises to increase your trust and faith in God. As you begin to do daily affirmations, you may not always believe that things are going to get better, or that God is going to see you through. But when you speak God's Word out loud to yourself, heaven will come down and things will change. As a result, when the winds and hail storms of life come, you will become immovable and untouched. The Word of God is alive and active. It shifts atmospheres and it causes things to work out in your favor. Most of all, God honors His Word above His name. He has not forgotten the words He has spoken over you. In Isaiah 55:11 (NIV), the Bible says, "So is my word that goes out from my mouth: It will not return to me empty but will accomplish what I desire and achieve the purpose for which I sent it." In Isaiah 55:12 (NIV), God says, "You will go out in joy and be led forth in peace."

So be encouraged, because in due time, you will see the harvest, blessings, healing, and breakthrough you have been waiting for. In the meantime, do not underestimate the power of your words, today. ***Joyce Meyers says it like this: "Line up your language with the heart of God, and enjoy the sweet, delightful healing it brings!"*** Speak words of life to promote a happy and peaceful day. Today, encourage yourself in the Lord and be made whole. Rely on Jesus to be your everything and He will make everything better for you.

PRAYER OF AFFIRMATIONS:

(This is an example of a daily affirmation prayer I have made. Ask the Lord what affirmations and biblical truths, He would like for you to speak over yourself. Then, be encouraged to create your own daily affirmations. Feel free to use this as a template.)

"I am affirmed in God's love for me. I am a child of God. I am beautifully, fearfully, and wonderfully made. God's love for me is based on who I am and not what I do. I am thriving in God's love and do not have to strive for it through my works. I am a child of God and not just a servant. Everything I place my hands on will be blessed and successful. The Lord Jesus has set me free and I am walking in the fullness of authority, power, and victory He has for me. Today is going to be a great day full of blessings, joy, peace, and God's daily surprises for me. I have rest in Jesus and no matter what comes my way, my peace will not be disturbed. Jesus is my rock, my fortress, the One I depend on, and the supplier of my needs. Yesterday is gone, today is here and I will see the goodness of the Lord in the land of the living. My spirit, body, mind, and soul are healed in Jesus' name. My family, loved ones, and I are protected under the blood of Jesus. I declare for the glory of the Lord to be revealed in my life. I am walking under an open heaven, so Lord may your blessings fall mightily upon me and my family. May I always be in the right position to receive those blessings. I will choose to love everyone and to share God's love, grace, patience, and His compassion towards everyone I encounter. Thank you for your mercies that are new every morning and great is your faithfulness towards me, Lord. The work God has begun in my life, He will bring it to pass. I stand in position this day to receive all you have for me, Lord. Lord, please remove every aggravation and scheme of the enemy, in Jesus' name. Every trap the devil has planned for me and for my family, will all fail. I am victorious. I am more than a conqueror. I am the head and not the tail, above and not beneath, a lender and not a borrower. I am prosperous, bold, and dearly loved. I declare all these words of truth will come to pass in my life, in Jesus' name, I pray, Amen."

Devotion 3: God's Love

"God's love for us is immeasurable. He shows us the way we should love others: unconditionally, without biases, and from a pure heart." - Laurine Voltaire

God is the originator and the author of love. We love because He first loved us (1 John 4:19 NIV). When we put God's love first in our hearts and first in our lives, and when we decide to walk in His love, we will have a successful and victorious life. God's love allows us to see life more clearly. We are able to make wiser decisions with the help of His love, and we are able to live peaceably with our neighbors. The Bible says in Luke 10:27 (ESV), "You shall love the Lord your God with all your heart, and with all your soul, and with all your strength, and with all your mind, and your neighbor as yourself." I believe Jesus was showing us the order of love. First, we need to learn how to love God and to be loved by God. Second, we need to learn how to love ourselves, and third, we need to learn how to love our neighbors.

God is love and the only way for you to learn how to love Him, I believe, is by allowing Him to love on you. In order to receive God's love, you will have to open your heart, entirely to Him. Once you know what it means to be unconditionally loved by God, you will then learn how to love yourself, which is a mandate for life. We are flawed, imperfect, sinful human beings that have been found worthy of God's marvelous love. ***God loves us just the way we are and His love changes us and makes us better people.*** For some of you today, in order for you to love yourself, you are going to have to release yourself from self-condemnation and forgive yourself of past mistakes and choices. God's love will help you to live a life empowered by the cross; a life without guilt, shame, blame, and judgment.

If you have never experienced the love of God or you want to receive more of it, I would encourage you to take some time to drench yourself in His presence to receive a fresh embrace from Him. Pastor Rick Warren puts it like this: "God's love is like an ocean. You can see its beginning, but not its end". God's love for you is never-failing. He wants you to dive into His never-ending sea of love and when you do, you will be made new. In His love, you will receive peace for your mind, hope for the day, joy in the midst of sorrow, and calmness for your soul. So be encouraged, to get enough of this love for yourself so that you can be His ambassador of love in all the earth. When you learn to love you for you, you will learn to love others for what they have to offer too. You will see people through the lenses of God's love and you will treat them the way they deserve to be treated. As you choose to love others with the selfless love of God, the power of His love within you will change the world.

<u>PRAYER:</u>

"Father, teach me your love. Help me to understand your love for me. Lord, I want to love myself the way you love me. Today I choose to give myself grace for my imperfections and for my mistakes, for in you alone Lord, I am being made perfect. Give me the grace to love others the way you love them. Jesus, I want more of you in every way. Fill the empty places of my heart and soul. I want for you Father, to always be more than enough for me.

Lord, I want to be your ambassador of love here on earth. I will not always get it right, but Jesus, help me to see others the way you see them, and help me to speak, interact, and face conflict with people the way you would. Give me grace and patience with my family members, children, spouse, friends, and co-workers. Let my days always honor you, Lord. Let the meditations of my heart and the words of my mouth be pleasing unto you, Lord, my Rock and my Redeemer. I want to be the fresh aroma of King Jesus everywhere I set my feet, so the world will know you and love you. In Jesus' name, I pray, Amen."

Devotion 4: Draw Near So You Can Hear

"When you draw near to God you will hear Him more clearly, and when you come closer to God, He will come closer to you." – Laurine Voltaire

"Draw near to God and He will draw near unto you."- James 4:8 (ESV)

Drawing near to God commences with our intentional act of setting apart quality time for Him. This is a time when we deliberately silence all the noise, to give a listening ear, and an open heart to our heavenly Father. **We are purposefully seeking God's face, just because we want to be with Him.** Many of us, at times, may think God is not speaking but the truth is, we are not taking the time to listen. Revelation 2:7 (NIV) says, "Whoever has ears, let them hear what the Spirit says." God speaks to His children in many ways. He can use external methods by speaking through your friends, through nature, or even through a sign on the freeway. God can speak through His Word, and He can even speak through the mouth of a child.

You should never despise the method God will use to speak to you. I believe God speaks to you according to how you will best receive His words. I also believe God speaks to you according to how your brain is wired. For example, to an engineer, God may use a mechanical design to speak to them and to an artist God may use a painting or piece of music. God can also internally download the message He wants to convey to your mind through a picture, or vision. Or, He will speak right to your heart, where you may feel an overwhelming sense of His love. Whatever way God chooses to convey His message to you, this encounter will change your life forever.

In my opinion, almost all believers have a deep longing within their souls to have God's presence be near to them, and for His voice to be ever-present, and very audible. Sometimes, God's voice can sound as clear as day and then other times, it can seem very distant. Often times, His voice can sound like a faint whisper, and it can be hard to decipher whether it is your own spirit or conscious speaking, or whether it is God. Overall, trying to discern the voice of God will take time. While you are going through this process of discernment, remember God loves you, and He will teach you how to hear Him more clearly.

Every so often, there can be hindrances and distractions in your life that try to keep you from getting close to God. Here are just a few hinderances:

1. Several of you may feel like God is distant from you when, in fact, you have pulled yourself away from His presence to some capacity. Other things in life have grasped, pulled, and have captivated your attention away from God. You cannot hear Him like you used to because there is something blocking you. Anything that tries to take the place of God in your life is a distraction sent by the enemy and it is your job to discern it and then get rid of it.

2. Some of you do not know how to relate to our heavenly Father because of the absence of an earthly Father. You may not know how to speak to God, or worse, you do not know how to be loved by Him. You need to open your heart to

receive God's truth that you are adopted into the family of Christ. Once you open your heart, God will free your life from all abandonment issues.

3. Lastly, some of you have a fear of being rejected by God because you feel shameful in His presence. The truth is we have all sinned and fall short of the glory of God (Romans 3:23 ESV). 1 John 1:9 (NIV) says, "If we confess our sins to the Lord, He is faithful and just to forgive us, and to cleanse us of all unrighteousness." We all have our inner struggles that we warfare with daily, that try to keep us from drawing near to God. God has given us Jesus and through the blood of Christ, we have the authority to fight back. His blood has given us the power to rebuke rejection and fear so that we can unashamedly and boldly enter into His gates with thanksgiving, and into His courts with praise. So, once you conquer your internal battles, you will be able to hear and discern God's voice more frequently.

It is your responsibility to arrest these strongholds in the Spirit by revoking their authority over you, to grant God full access and authority over your life.

In Robert Morris' book, *Frequency: Tune In. Hear God*, he says: **"Hearing God's voice is not about something we do. Rather, hearing God is about someone we are. Hearing God is not primarily a behavior. It's a reflection of our identity. We hear God because of who we are and because of whose we are."** The more you draw near to God by spending time with Him in prayer, reading the Bible, and by soaking (a.k.a. sitting) in silence before the Lord, He will become more evident to you. It is a guarantee that you will begin to hear His voice more and more. You see, when you come near to God, you find out the secrets of His heart. He begins to confide in you. He will give you wisdom and revelation for your life, and you will receive inner healing, and a restored faith to trust in the Almighty Savior again. God is calling you to go a little deeper in this day. Just tarry in His presence and allow Him to saturate your soul. He is bringing you back to Himself on eagles' wings, like He did for the people of Israel (Exodus 19:4).

So, let me encourage you with these words: the mere fact that you want to be closer to God means you are heading down the right path. Just anchor your hope towards God, and keep paddling towards that distant shore of faith, even if you are unsure of what you might encounter or see. Know that Jesus will meet you wherever you are. As you continue to draw nearer to God, the waves will get bumpy and the trials of life will come like earthquakes, with full intention to shake your ground and to knock you down. But, as long as you keep your anchor secured in Christ, you will see that He will never let you down.

For those who have run away, turn back to God, your first love. Join me in being caught in the net of God's love where He will lift you high out of the mighty waters, for He will never let you drown. Let Him speak peace and gentle melodies over your soul. Today take a step of faith and be brave to come before the throne of grace, even in the face of adversity. When you need God the most, He will always be there for you. So be encouraged to draw near to God, for He's already in your midst. Open your heart and just believe it.

PRAYER:

"Father God, I want to draw near to you and I want to know you more. I want to see you face to face and know your heart. Teach me, Lord, to know your voice, to discern between your Spirit, the enemy, and my own thoughts. Help me to hear you so clearly like Samuel did as a child when you called his name while he was sleeping. (1 Samuel 3) I want to hear you like Moses did when you called his name from the burning bush (Exodus 3), and like Peter did when you called him to step out on faith to walk on the troubled waters (Matthew 14:22-33). Thank you for being with me now, Lord, through all the trials of life and through the calamity the enemy brings. Thank you for putting a fight in me to never give up chasing after your presence. Thank you that nothing can take me away from your presence. Father, bless me with the awareness to know your voice so that I can hear you more clearly in this season I am in. Grant me the patience to wait in your presence to hear you speak to me. I open my heart for you to come in. Everything that is hindering me from hearing your voice, I bind it and rebuke it away from me, in Jesus' name, to the place of no return. I am free to listen to you my God, to receive clear wisdom and guidance from you. I am free to draw nearer to you, and I am free to be healed by you. In Jesus' name, Amen."

Devotion 5: Developing A Culture of Rest

"God, you have made us for yourself, and our hearts are restless till they find their rest in you." - Augustine

When I think about resting, I think about laying down at the beach with a fruity drink in my hand, as I am listening to the waves crash back and forth on the shoreline. For most of you, this image is the epitome of rest; getting away for a week, with nothing to worry about, no phone calls or work to bother you, it's just you and the waves. *How many of you know, that the rest you are longing for is much greater than a vacation in Orlando or an adventure in an African safari? The rest you are yearning for is the Sabbath rest.*

For most Christians, Sunday is the day they set apart to be their Sabbath. Keeping the Sabbath day holy is one of the Ten Commandments found in Exodus 20:8. Christians have been following God's footsteps in practicing the Sabbath for centuries. After God created the world, "on the seventh day God finished His work that He had done, and He rested on the seventh day from all His work that He had done" (Genesis 2:2 ESV). This is a wonderful discipline we all should have: ceasing from all sorts of work in order to reflect on the goodness of God in our lives. Sadly, Sunday for some of us is no longer the day where we rest, but it is the day we get last minute errands done and it is the day to make the most money during work hours, (a.k.a. "time-and-a-half"). Now, instead of resting, we are busier than ever.

If we do not take time to stop working, we will miss what God is doing. If God stopped to rest, then we should. Resting in God as I mentioned before, is a command and not a suggestion. In Hebrews 4:9 (NIV), the Bible talks about another Sabbath-rest that remains for the people of God. I believe this is an everyday encounter with the eternal rest of Jesus that is only found in the Father's presence. When we find this Sabbath rest in God, we are finding rest for our souls, rest that gives us a transformative mindset, and a re-energized heart. One of the points of having a Sabbath is to help re-align our perception of our own lives to God's perception of our lives.

Weekly Sabbaths are important in all aspects and there are numerous reasons why we should do it. The Sabbath is the day where we can lay all our burdens at the feet of Jesus, as Matthew 11:28 (NKJV) instructs us to do: "Come to me all you who labor and are heavy laden, *and burdened* and I will give you rest." *The Sabbath is the day where the heart of humanity finds rest in the heart of their Creator.* It allows us to remember what God has done and to be grateful for what He is going to do. When we rest, we receive God's truth for our lives. I like to imagine it like this: when we take time to rest in God, it is like we are being transported back to the Garden of Eden in the cool of the day. God's presence comes to walk with us, and He imparts truth into our weary hearts to keep us hopeful for a better tomorrow in Him. I believe God is developing a culture of Sabbath rest in the hearts, lifestyles, and the minds of His people.

Observing the Sabbath lets us rest in the Father's love for us. When we rest, we also find out that our works do not make God love us any more than He already does. His love for us is not performance-based. Also, weekly Sabbaths allow us to be ministered to after a long hard-worked week of pouring into the lives of others. We are always taking care of others but it is time for us to learn to take care of ourselves. Taking care of ourselves is not selfish because self-care is necessary. When we do this, it will help us to deal with some of our undealt emotions, traumas, and frustrations with life. Sometimes we can be so consumed with being busy that we just sweep conflict, offenses, and our emotional wounds under the rug, instead of dealing with them head-on. These self-reflective moments will help us to apply the life-lessons we often give to others and use them to get ourselves emotionally, physically, and spiritually stable. When we build a culture of Sabbath in our own lives, we can then enjoy life to its fullest. Furthermore, when we are rested, we can invite those around us to learn how to Sabbath as well, which builds a culture of rest in community.

I believe God longs to carry you into His resting place; a place full of contentment and satisfying peace. So be encouraged, to take time to rest this week, so that you can truly witness and experience what it means to Sabbath with the Almighty. Resting for everyone will look different. You can rest by reflecting on God's power and majesty by praying, reading a book, doing something adventurous such as hiking, catching up on sleep, enjoying your favorite past time, or simply just having good fun with loved ones. On your next Sabbath day, choose to vacation with your heavenly Father by pitching a tent, hanging up your hammock, or just lounging on your lawn chair, as you reflect and gaze in amazement at the wonderful things He has done.

<u>PRAYER:</u>

"Father, I thank you and I accept your invitation of rest. Lord, I want to find eternal rest within your presence. Let me never be too busy to see your goodness towards me each day. Give me the grace to balance everything you have given me to do. Jesus, I release from my life everything that is not supposed to be my responsibility. Help me to sustain a peaceful attitude in living for you and in serving others. I lay every burden down at your feet. I lay down my busy mind, I lay down my family, I lay down my career, and I lay down my education and degrees. Lord, I lay down all of me. God, just as you rested on the seventh day reflecting on all you have made, give me the wisdom to do the same. I want to reflect on all the good you have blessed me with, always counting my blessings, for I am grateful for each and every one of them. In Jesus' name, I pray, Amen."

Devotion 6: I Am A Child of God

"For you have not received a spirit of slavery leading again to fear [of God's judgment], but you have received the Spirit of adoption as sons [the Spirit producing sonship] by which we [joyfully] cry, "Abba! Father!" The Spirit Himself testifies and confirms together with our spirit [assuring us] that we [believers] are children of God. And if [we are His] children, [then we are His] heirs also: heirs of God and fellow heirs with Christ [sharing His spiritual blessing and inheritance], if indeed we share in His suffering so that we may also share in His glory." – Romans 8:15-17 (AMP)

"I am a child of God." What does that really mean? As simple as it sounds, trying to understand what it means, can be a little bit complicated. I believe it means God or Abba in heaven is your Father, you are His child, and He loves you. Sadly, the essence of what it means to be a child of God has been distorted and abused over the years. Some Christians believe that when you are a child of God, you purely work for God. This is called a Master and servant relationship. God is the Master and His children are His servants, or in other words, God is the employer and you are His laborer.

For Christians that hold this view, this is what their typical "work" week as a child of God would look like: 1) you pray at least an hour a day, 2) you make sure you do community outreach, 3) you evangelize and share the gospel, 4) you try your best to show godly compassion to people, placing others above yourself, 5) you tithe and give a love offering to the missions committee, 6) you fast at least once a week, 7) you are faithful to your spouse and care for your children or, if you are single, you live a life of purity. All these things are noble activities we can aspire to do as Christians because they are all biblically sound. However, our relationship with God is not based on conditional works but on unconditional love. We aim to do good works because we love God, and not because we are trying to be loved by Him. If we measure our relationship with God and our value in His eyes, by the things we do, then we are going about it all wrong. It is as if we are trying to attain righteousness through our actions when we have already been made righteous through Jesus' blood. We were not created to earn God's love; we were created to receive it.

Some of us are striving to be loved by God, instead of just knowing we are loved by God. Can you relate to this? I sure can. *You may be trying to capture God's attention when you already have it or you are trying to get Him to notice you when you are always on His mind. You do not have to do anything to pay for God's love or prove that you belong to God.* I am not encouraging you to stop doing good deeds to glorify God. That is not my point. My point is this: none of us can give God anything that He does not already have. Me being a child of God and you being a child of God is only based on one work and that is the act of the cross. Once again, I am not encouraging you to live a life without prayer and reading the Word. These two disciplines are necessary for you to engage in, in order for you to get closer to God. What I am simply emphasizing is that, we need to relearn what it means to just be a daughter or son of God, to fully rest in this identity. And we need to learn how to receive the abundance of love that He has for us.

So today, rethink your theology of what qualifies and distinguishes you as a child of God. If you think that God is impressed with what you have done for Him so far and if you think your good deeds are going to make Him love you more, you have been misled. ***You are loved by God because you are lovable, and He chose to make you His child.*** God is not like us. He does not need to find one likable thing about a person's character in order to love them. Every moment of every day, He willingly chooses to love you and that means all of you. In Ephesians 1:5 (NLT) the Bible says, "God decided in advance to adopt us into his own family by bringing us to himself through Jesus Christ. This is what He wanted to do, and it gave Him great pleasure." God is pleased to call you His son or His daughter. This makes God happy. God wanted you to be a part of His family before you were even born. You have been engrafted into this family and there is nothing that can separate you from His love. As God's child, you are an heir to His kingdom and an heir to everything that belongs to Him. Remember, all the Father has is yours. This includes His everlasting peace, blessings upon blessings, over-bubbling joy, and dominion and authority on this earth. You shall possess everywhere God settles your feet.

I know learning to just be a son of God or a daughter of God is hard for some of you, because the only parental relationship you may have ever known is broken, and they are not the best influence or role model. Your parents cannot be compared to a holy God. They will never measure up and where they fell short God will rise to the occasion. So be encouraged, to challenge yourself to walk in your identity as God's child with boldness and confidence. It is a journey of transformation and elevation. Allow God to transform your mind, heart, and character to be like Christ Jesus. This path is about learning and knowing Whose you are as a favored and beloved child of the Most High God. So, own it, know it, believe in it, and just be it.

PRAYER:

"Thank you, Father, that you have called me as your own. Lord, teach me what it means to be your child. Help me to know and to possess my rightful place as a child of God. I want to walk in your integrity and in your likeness. Change my mindset from any wrongful teachings, I have believed in the past and teach me your ways. I want to know you, Lord, and I want to be who you have called me to be. Help me to just be your child. Father, please teach me about your love and teach me how to love myself. Lord, let not my works be performance-based but Christ-centered. Break every privileged or entitlement mindset that I may have. All that I have and all that I am is because of your grace and favor upon my life. I am a child of God because you have called me your own. I pray that all that I do for your glory is done in full-participation with the Holy Spirit. In Jesus' name, I pray, Amen."

PART 2.

Gods Daily Provisions:

Hope, Faith, Love, And Forgiveness In Christ

.

Devotion 7: For Your Sake, Learn to be Happy

Yesterday is gone and today is here. When you leave the sorrows of yesterday in the past, you make room in your heart to believe in God again, for a better today and for an even more joyous tomorrow. - Laurine Voltaire

Charles Spurgeon says: "God made human beings as He made His other creatures to be happy. They are in their right element when they are happy." I strongly concur with this statement that God desires for us to be happy and it is our right to be happy. However, for some of us, every time we want to be happy and optimistic about life, the pains of our hearts try to remind us to not let our guard down. When we want to move forward into the goodness God has for us, our emotions are like an alarm clock, knowing just when to remind us of the agony we have recently undergone. Even though we know we should be happy, our hearts have a funny way of cautioning our minds to come back to reality, reminding us of everything that is possibly going wrong with our lives.

In spite of what you are personally going through, I want to encourage you to put a smile on your face, because no matter what this day may bring God has ordered your steps and as you continue to wait on Him, God promises that He will work things out for you (Isaiah 64:4). David says in Psalm 27:13 (NIV), "I remain confident of this: I will see the goodness of the LORD in the land of the living." You will live and see that there is something good in this day for you. If you keep holding onto hope and assuring yourself that God is in control of your days and it is not a matter of luck or karma, you will live to see God's goodness and joy that is waiting for you. In Psalm 16:11 (ESV) the Bible says, "In your presence is the fullness of joy."

If you change your mindset and command your heart to bless the Lord, you might just have an awesome day. A lot of times we tend to have bad days because, we choose to spend our days complaining about the things we don't have, instead of being thankful for the things we do have. I believe thankfulness is one of the keys to happiness. Life may want you to live in misery, but God wants you to live in peace. Misery may love company but declare today that it can no longer be your friend. For today, you choose to befriend happiness, peace, joy, and hope. Peace shall be your cup this morning, joy shall be your everlasting spring bubbling up in your spirit as a well of life, and hope shall be your strong support.

Today, seize every opportunity that comes your way as a divine appointment from the Lord. These divine encounters are His ways of showing you how He has fashioned this day for you to be over-joyed. *Trust God and be happy, so you can start learning to live life for yourself instead of having life live you.* Decide for yourself what type of day you want to have and believe in God that it will be just that. If bad things are happening keep pressing on and pray for the Lord to open your eyes to see where His hand is at work, and where the devil is plotting a scheme. Let God expand your thinking by allowing Him to download His good thoughts into your mind so His thoughts can become your reality.

So be encouraged, to believe that the impossibilities of life are being made possible, the hard things are becoming easier, and the imperfections of life are being made perfect for you in Christ. My prayer for you, is to be happy, joyful, and content while you're walking the streets of life with Jesus, hand in hand. Enjoy as you both are singing a new song of praise together, dancing to the beat of never-ending joy, skipping in freedom, while leaping in grace. Rejoice, my friend. Know God is good and He has been good to you. For your sake, be happy and motivate yourself to be delighted in your God. You have been down for too long and it is time to get up and take the day by force. God has brought you from a mighty long way, He is taking you from glory to glory, and He is working it all out in your favor. Now, those are things to be happy about. I believe today is going to be a good day because you serve a great God.

Laurine Voltaire

<u>PRAYER:</u>

"Lord, today I thank you for the joy that is coming my way. I choose to be happy, content, and satisfied in all you have for me. Teach me what it means to be happy in you. Jehovah Shammah (*The Lord is there*) you are in each day waiting right there for me to meet you. Be my guiding light and help me to see your goodness in even the worst of times. I pray against having a pessimistic mindset and I pray that my thoughts will be the thoughts of Christ. I command my soul to trust in the Lord, for He is faithful. I command my heart to pant after the streams of God, for there, I will find living water. I command my mind to focus its attention on Christ and to not get distracted. I command my emotions to yearn for godly things, pure things, and for the will of the Father. Heavenly Father, I want to long for the things you desire for me to have. Thank you, Jesus, that every day in you is and will be a good and happy day. In Jesus' name, I pray, Amen."

Devotion 8: Ask and You Shall Receive

"God does not give us everything we want, but He does fulfill His promises, leading us along the best and straightest paths to Himself." – Dietrich Bonhoeffer

As you go through the course of your day, what are the things that you tend to gravitate towards as your source of comfort and peace? What are the things that you lean on when your boss and coworkers get on your nerves, when your children are not listening, or when you are just having one of those days? Your first choice should always be drawing near to the Lord so that He can be your strength, your help, and your peace. However, instead of choosing God we tend to choose so many other things in this life. For instance, when you have a bad break up, do you run to prayer or to a bowl of ice cream and a good movie to sob to? When you are angry and are fed up with life, do you run to God with your problems or do you pick up the phone and call your best friend? For most of us, we know that God's comfort is incomparable, and we know, that He alone can provide the answer to our problems.

But still, we are hesitant and we do not turn to God first. I believe there are a number of reasons why we do this. Well for starters, it is easier to run to things that are tangible, such as, a friend or a lover, who will give you a big hug and a shoulder to cry on, and it is easier to run to things that will give you a temporary satisfaction like smoking or engaging in sexual pleasures. Also, it is much easier to wallow in your misery, than it is to ask God for help on how to get out. Some of you may have a fear of being disappointed, if God does not change your situation the way you think it should be changed. Lastly, there are some of you that do not ask God for anything, because you are fearful, that you will not receive a favorable answer from Him.

My motto is: "If you never ask then you will never know." Prayer is not for God; it is for us. Prayer is the way for us to communicate and to find God. It is the place where God is able to pour His love into our hearts. So, instead of just talking about what you are going through to everybody you know, invite God in, so He can move on your behalf, change your circumstance, and impart His love into your heart. I am not saying you shouldn't have good friends to lean on in times of need. I am suggesting for all of us to try something new and healthy, and this is to try God first. There is a reason why His name is Jehovah Shalom: *The Lord Who sends peace.* I believe God is waiting to send peace into our situations, but He is waiting for us to ask. There is a powerful, yet simplistic kingdom principle found in Matthew 7:7 (ESV), "Ask and it will be given to you." You may not have a resolution to your problems and you may not have peace for your current storms, because you are not inquiring of the Lord. You are trying to do life in your strength instead of relying on Jesus.

I believe God is always willing to give you answers to your prayers because He is a good, good, Father. There is a reason why Jesus tells us in the Bible, to ask Him for things we need and want. Our heavenly Father is waiting patiently to bless us. I believe God is waiting for us to ask Him for help, guidance, and for solutions. By doing this, our hearts will grow fond in trusting that He will provide. When you ask the Lord for something and you wait for Him to fulfill it, there is a hope that begins to grow in your heart, and you begin to believe that God will establish the very thing He has promised. God has an impeccable track record and the same way He provided for you in the past He is more than able to do it again. Also, after you pray and release your heart to God, there is a peace that comes upon you that Paul speaks about in Philippians 4:7 (AMP): "The peace of God [that peace that reassures the heart, that peace] which transcends all understanding, that peace] which stands guard over your hearts and minds in Christ Jesus is yours."

So be encouraged, to continue to pray to the Lord for all things, because in Mark 11:24 (NIV) the Bible says, "Therefore I tell you, whatever you ask for in prayer, believe that you have received it, and it will be yours". You may not get what you are asking for from God right away, but it is coming in God's timing and He will bless you according to His perfect will for you. Still remain anticipative and thankful that your God has everything you need in the palm of His hands and He is ready and willing to give it to you. The same God that did not spare His own Son but graciously gave you Jesus, "Will He not give you so much more: all things including His good promises for you?" (Romans 8:32).

God is a loving Father, and those who ask in faith and in expectancy, will receive an abundance of His good treasures. A grace without measure.

<u>PRAYER:</u>

"Thank you, Lord, for I know when I ask of you, I will receive from you. Thank you, in advance for answering all my prayers. Please increase my hope, peace, and confidence in you. I will wait for your sovereign will to be done in my life. Lord, I believe you will supply all of my needs and bless me in due time. Help me, Lord, to run to you first as my source of help when I am desperate. I pray that you will quench every thirst of my soul and spirit. Teach me to depend on you, Lord, to know you are my deliverer, my help, and a good friend that sticks close by me in every season, for you will never change. In Jesus' name, I pray, Amen."

Devotion 9: Having All You Need and Then Some

"Do not look back on happiness or dream of it in the future. You are only sure of today; do not let yourself be cheated out of it." – Henry Ward Beecher

Do you ever feel like you just do not have enough in life? You do not have enough money, you do not have enough joy, you do not have enough time, you do not have enough friends, and the list goes on and on. When we go through life pointing out all the things that we do not have, we tend to feel like our lives are half complete. The reality is, we, as God's children, "lack *nothing* and no good thing" (Psalm 34:10 ESV). *If Jesus is supposed to be more than enough for all of us, than why is it hard for us to accept that He is our all-sufficient Savior?* I think the battle begins when we become constantly discontented with life. Maybe we need to stop comparing our lives to others and start trusting in God's timing to bless us. We need to change our thinking from looking at the glass half empty to looking at it half full. *When we change our negative or "stinking thinking" to being more positive and optimistic, we become more appreciative and grateful for what God has done for us.*

Since the beginning of time, God always desired for us to live a happy life. In Psalms 144:15 (ESV) the Bible says, "Blessed are the people whose God is the Lord". In the Hebrew, "Blessed" in this passage translates to, "Happy are the people whose God is the Lord". So no matter what you have been going through, you have something to be happy about today. You have the most precious possession in all the world. You have God as your Lord. He is the Lord who will lead you in every direction of life, so you will never be lost. He is the One who will provide for you, so you will never be without. And He is the One who comforts you and keeps you, so you will always be safe and loved. You are very special to God.

God's plan for humanity's happiness started in Genesis chapter 2:15 when God placed man in a garden called Eden. Eden was a garden filled with all kinds of plants, fruits, trees, and nourishment for humanity. Eden had everything we could ever imagine and then some. In ancient Hebrew, Eden means "delight" and it also means "pleasurable". God placed His people in a home which was delightful and pleasurable in every way. These pleasures were godly pleasures, things that were fulfilling to the spirit, mind, soul, and body. What more could mankind ask for? You see, you and I are not meant to live a life of poverty, sadness, and depression. A life struggling every month, living from paycheck to paycheck, barely making ends meet, working hard to only pay our bills, barely seeing our children or our spouses, while not being able to have fun and do leisure activities with our loved ones. In Psalm 16:11, God showed David a revelation of life and how life is supposed to be. In this passage, David writes, "You have made known to me the path of life; in Your presence is the fullness of joy, and at Your right hand, are pleasures forevermore" (Psalm 16: 11 ESV). All that we are looking for and seeking for in this life is found in the presence of God. Our sense of happiness, contentment, and fulfillment in all aspects of our daily living is found right here in God's presence. And just like God had treasures for Adam and Eve in the garden, God has treasures for you here on earth as well, and they are called pleasures forevermore. Pleasures of seeing your passions fulfilled and seeing the desires of your heart come to pass. Once God becomes your everything and your One true delight is in Him, you will discover He is truly all you really need.

God is our all-sufficient Provider and He has equipped us with the ability to make wealth. So, if you want to see productivity in your life, you need to start using what's inside of you. God has given you gifts, talents, and abilities that will make room for you and they will bring you before great men (Proverbs 18:16). You are favored by the Lord. As God's child, you are called to thrive and soar on wings as eagles through all that comes your way. Once you use what is in you to bring glory to His kingdom, there will be an overflowing of grace poured over your life, thus attracting the blessings of God to you. It won't always happen instantly, for not everyone is meant to be an overnight sensation. It will take diligence, perseverance, and, most of all, trusting in the Lord. Seek first the kingdom of God: His agenda, His culture, His power, His way of living, and then all these other things that you want, will be added unto you (Matthew 6:33).

So be encouraged child of God, for you are called to be blessed, live in abundance, and prosper. You have the ability to be prosperous not just with money, but most importantly in your calling, in your relationships and in your emotional well-being. You can be prosperous and bountiful in using your talents and gifts to help empower others. In fact, once you understand that you are called to be blessed, your mindset will change and instead of allowing the world and its toils to change you, you will stand to change the world. So be encouraged today, for you are not called to just survive, but to thrive! And know that you can do all things through Christ who gives you strength (Philippians 4:13 NLT).

Say it with me, "I CAN DO ALL THINGS THROUGH CHRIST WHO GIVES ME STRENGTH!"

PRAYER:

"Thank you, Jesus, for always providing for me. Help me to trust in your provisions for my life, not just financially but in all things. Teach me your ways, oh Lord. Jesus, I pray you will always be more than enough for me. Lead me in your path of life, where in your presence there is the fullness of joy, and in your right-hand, pleasures forevermore. As I am waiting on you Lord and taking steps to move forward, help me to be thankful for the provisions of the now and trust in you for the provisions of tomorrow. In Jesus' name, I pray, Amen."

Devotion 10: Living Purposely

"Wonderful changes are going to happen in your life as you begin to live it on purpose"- Rick Warren

Choosing to live your life on purpose, for a purpose, begins with training your mind, attitude, and emotions to be constantly aware of this simple truth: you are alive for a reason. The mere fact that you are alive, is evidence that God has great things in store for you. Sadly, most people do not even know why they are here. You may be one of them. You may be on a constant mission, trying to discover how to fulfill your purpose. Well, the only way you are going to figure out your calling, is by spending time in God's presence and in the Word. In these precious moments, God will show you the plans He has for your life. He will reassure you, that you are on the right track or He will redirect your steps to be in alignment with His will. At this very moment, if you are discouraged and if you are tempted to throw in the towel, be encouraged to not give up on yourself and do not give up on God. He has not counted you out of this race. Remember, if you decide to give up, there will be a void in the earth, in the space you were made to occupy.

No one else on this earth can be who God has called you to be, because your purpose, was specifically designed with you in mind. "Eyes have not seen, and ears have not heard, and it has not entered into the heart of man, all that God has prepared for those who love

Him" (1 Corinthians 2:9 NAS). You should be encouraged to take every day that you wake up as a sign, that there is a need for you here on earth. There is someone in need of what God has placed inside of you. You are valuable and irreplaceable. **You are a gift to mankind.**

Living life on purpose, for a purpose, can be a wonderful learning experience. I have learned that God places exceptional desires deep within our hearts and as we grow in Him, He will cause these things to come to life. I believe God has given us His compassion towards all people and He uses us as His vessels, to spread His love to a broken and dying world. Whatever your heart tends to gravitate to and love, these are the things I believe, are a part of your purpose and calling. Therefore, if you have a passion in your heart for things like feeding the poor, praying for the sick, visiting inmates in prison, and seeking justice for the oppressed, this is evidence that God has given you the concerns of His heart (Matthew 25:40-45 NIV).

You may not feel qualified to be called or used by God, but remember God uses those who are disqualified, and He qualifies them by His grace. He uses those who feel unworthy and He builds His name within them and causes them to become great (read the story of Gideon found in Judges 6). So, do not wait for something extraordinary to happen to you before you start living your life on purpose. There are many ways you can go about making an impact in this world including joining a ministry at your church, volunteering at a non-profit organization, or simply sharing your life experiences with others. Testify to the nations about how God has delivered you from your hardships and struggles, and let them know about your triumphs and victories. Tell them, about how God has brought you through, and kept you, and healed you. Your story will give them a source of strength and confidence to believe in God like never before.

Sharing your faith with others who have lost hope is your way of making the world a better place. When you make it, others will believe they will too. When you keep choosing to fight in spite of all you have been through, others will keep fighting too. When you say "Yes!" to living and "No!" to dying, you are creating a legacy of hope without even knowing it. People are depending on you to live. Remember when you can't, God can. Do not allow doubt and confusion, your pain from your past, and your own insecurities of thinking you are not good enough, discourage you anymore. **Let that place of pain motivate and propel you into your future.**

My prayer for you today, is that God will raise you up to the same level of thinking as Christ. I pray He will expand your capacity to achieve what you thought was unachievable and to attain what you thought was unattainable. I pray you will embrace your identity in Christ. There is a reason why you are different. Just be you. Accept your uniqueness of being the daughter or the son of the King. Know that you are God's prized possession. He boldly and unashamedly wants to share you with this world as His perfected light; to shine you into the lives of others. So be encouraged, to deliberately live your life with purpose, on purpose, and for a purpose.

<u>PRAYER:</u>

"Jesus, thank you for waking me up this morning. My purpose, my hope, and my life are all found in you. I want to fully live out my purpose here on earth in you Jesus. I surrender my life to you and declare this is your day to show me what I am created for. I choose your will over mine, and I willingly give you the rights to my life, so you can guide me to wherever you know is best. I believe you have the best plans for me. I believe your plans won't harm me, and I believe I have a hope and a future to look forward to in you. Help me to accept that your plans are better than mines. Today, I choose to live life as your beloved child. Help me to seize every opportunity you bring my way, as I walk in your favor. And Lord, I pray you will surprise me with your presence as I wait in expectation for you. Lord, please give me the boldness to share my story with someone else, so that they will also choose to live their life on purpose and for a purpose. In Jesus' name, I pray, Amen."

<u>Devotion 11: Overcoming Pain</u>

"Nothing paralyzes our lives like the attitude that things can never change. We need to remind ourselves that God can change things. Outlook determines outcome. If we see only the problems, we will be defeated; but if we see the possibilities in the problems, we can have victory." - Warren Wiersbe

If you could change your current state or condition, your lifestyle or the choices you have made, would you do so, or would you just leave everything as is? So many of you, if you had the chance, you would probably change just about everything in your life. You would change the way you look, your health, your finances, your job, the family you were born into, your friends, your marital status and the list goes on and on. Most of the things I have listed, if you really wanted to change them, you could. For instance, if you wanted to change your finances, you could just get a better job or if you wanted to change the way you look, you could just exercise and change your eating habits. But what do you do when you are faced with a problem that cannot be fixed by you or by the choices you make? How do you cope with the irreversible events that have happened in your life or with the things that will never change because they are out of your control? These include tragic situations such as the death of a loved one, the results of a traumatic car accident, or a childhood trauma.

How do you get past the pain? Will you ever be able to move on and move forward? When your life changes for the worst, in the blink of an eye, these questions may appear to be unanswerable. I know firsthand, that the only One who can give you solutions to your heart's content is Jesus Christ.

After my mother went on to be with the Lord in 2015, my first question to the Lord was, "Why?" I couldn't comprehend why God would allow something so devastating to happen to my family. My next question was concerning the pain I now had to bear, without my consent, and without warning. I often wondered, "Will it ever get better?" Of course, the pain in my heart answered God for me, screaming, "No way! Never! She is gone, she is gone forever, there is no coming back from it and you can never recover from this!" When you are stuck in a dark place, a place of grief and sadness, it will be hard to hear what God is trying to say to you. Like the psalmist David says in Psalm 88:18 (NIV), "Darkness is now your closest friend." Thankfully, in the darkest moments of your life, God's glory shines brightly. David says it best in Psalm 139:12 (NIV), "Even the darkness will not be dark to you; the night will shine like the day, for the darkness will shine as light to you". God is about to speak truth into your situation and into your heart, letting you know that everything will eventually get better, because He is in control. So, consider it pure joy when you suffer through many trials, brethren, for the break of dawn is coming and the Son is going to rise on your situations. For, although you cannot hear Him, or receive His words because of your pain, God is speaking, and His peaceful and powerful words will pierce and heal your soul. Through His grace and glory, He will reveal to you that this pain is a blessing in disguise.

Now, it may be hard for some of you to swallow what I just said because how can change that brings pain, be a blessing? *I do not know how God does it, but He truly has the gifted ability to cause all things to work together for your good. There is purpose in your pain.* Our sovereign God, in His love, will reveal this purpose to you. I do not know why things happen the way they do. I do not even believe God desires for us to suffer the way we do. ***But what I do know is that He will never allow your pain to go in vain.*** You will be healed from your pain. Through the marvelous works of God's hand in your life, your pain will become someone else's healing ground once they hear your story.

I used to believe that some pains never leave the soul and they leave you wounded for a lifetime. Now, I choose to believe that pain is only meant to be a temporary feeling, and God's healing power is eternal. I have been learning along the way, that God uses all things to work out for my good, even the worse events in my life. I decided to take the words in the Bible, as words of truth for my own life. For example, I believe God had me in mind as well, when He told the prophet Isaiah, to write these words to the people of Israel concerning their grief in captivity:

> "He will comfort all who mourn and provide for those who grieve, by giving them a crown of beauty instead of ashes, the oil of joy or a joyous blessing instead of mourning, and the garment of praise or festive praise instead of the spirit of despair." (Isaiah 61:2-3 NIV & NLT)

God wrote those words for me, because He knew once my mother passed away, I would be searching for answers to my pain. I also dare to believe that God had you in mind when He allowed those words to be written to help you face this loss, sudden death, accident, and sudden changes, head on with a heart full of faith. In this passage, God is saying there are remedies to replace pain, grief, despair, and mourning in your life and they are called comfort, beauty, joy, and praise. God wants you to feel joy in the midst of sorrow and He wants you to see beauty rising when all hope is dead. Jesus said in John 14:16 that He would ask the Father to send the Holy Spirit, who is also known as the Comforter, to be with His disciples. The Holy Spirit is accessible to everyone who believes, and He is here now ready and willing to comfort you.

Today, I believe God is extending an invitation for you to exchange your old ways of thinking about loss, grief, change, and tragic circumstances, to receive His new and fresh way of processing pain. You will be as Isaiah 61:3 (NIV) says, as "Oaks of righteousness, a planting of the Lord for the display of His splendor." You will be unshakable, unmovable, and standing tall, towering over your pain. For God is not calling you to stay down, but to rise up. Weeping may endure for the night, and I know those hours can appear to be unending, especially the hours from midnight to dawn, but guaranteed joy will come in the morning. It may not seem like it now, but your seasons of happiness, joy, praising, and dancing, are here. Give yourself grace to get to the other side of this. You are going to make it out strong.

Do not rush the process. There are necessary steps you will need to take when mourning a deceased loved one and when trying to recover from an injury, accident, or illness. These things will take time, much prayer, and wise counsel from those who can help lead you in the right direction. Allow the Lord to restore your heart. You must believe that God will never give you more than you can bear, and He will make a way out of it for you. He carries your burdens daily and you will never be crushed under the weight of your distress. You will make it through this. So, be encouraged to make room for joy to come into your heart and for happiness to ransom your soul. Once you do, you will smile again like never before. Be merry with cheer, for the Lord is turning it around for you.

<u>PRAYER:</u>

"Father, I give you my pain right now and I pray that you will heal my heart. I pray that you will relieve me from stress and heartache, in Jesus' name. I bind and rebuke the spirits of heaviness, despair, and grief in Jesus' name to the place of no return. I remove the clothing of heaviness and grief through the blood of Jesus, and I put on your garment of praise in Jesus' name. Teach me how to grieve in you Lord. There is nothing too hard for you Lord, and I pray you will reveal the purpose of this pain to me. Please, give me the accountability partners, prayer partners, and people who can help me through this process, because I know I am not supposed to be doing this alone. I receive your joy for me, your peace, your beauty, and your comfort. Holy Spirit, rest upon my mind and help me to live in your comfort. Teach me how to give myself grace as I am recovering from this pain. Thank you for being my source of strength. I pray I will not turn to my own methods of self-medication or self-healing. By your strength alone, I will not engage in any form of bingeing or sin that entertains the flesh, to feed into this pain anymore, in Jesus' name. I choose you, Jesus, to be the remedy of my soul and my refuge. You are my all in all, my everything, and my Healer. In Jesus' name, I pray, Amen."

Devotion 12: Living in Transparency

"We can only be our true, naked, and divine self in the presence of God." – Laurine Voltaire

"How are you doing today?" No really, besides the cliché answers of "I am well", or "It is well with my soul", I really want to know, "How are you doing?" I feel like that question is barely ever answered with an honest response. Society and culture have trained us to mask our feelings and emotions. We have been taught it is not proper to share how you are feeling because it is a sign of weakness. So, we bury our frustrations by working harder to become the best at what we do. Or, we exercise or engage in self-harm behaviors like drinking, having sex, doing drugs, or overeating, in order to avoid talking about what's going on inside our hearts. Despite what we have been taught, "Do you think it is appropriate to let your hair down, and be your true self in front of other people?" "Should you be able to comfortably bare your soul unto another?" Or, is it a shameful thing to share with someone that you are truly hurting on the inside?

I believe, sometimes, this sense of hesitancy in sharing our hearts stems from our inability to trust another human being with the most intricate parts of our lives. Why? Possibly the reason you are hurting in the first place, is because, another human being has left you heartbroken. Therefore, how can you expect to put your trust in another person, when you have been let down before? I think we also tend to shy away from sharing because we are scared others will perceive our sense of transparency as a sign of being fragile and easily broken. For some of you, you are afraid you will be rejected. As a result, you have mastered the ability to suppress your emotions in order to push through life and to get the job done. You are a pro at faking it until you make it. For some of you, that is the advice that someone has given you in order to survive the real world and you have made it your life's philosophy. But the reality is, you cannot survive the world, by tuning out your feelings or by becoming emotionally unattached with what is happening inside of you. *You will only begin to live life to its full measure when you share your true feelings as to how you are doing. It is normal not to be in a good place all the time. Most people are not. Just because you are not okay today, does not mean this is the determining factor of your everyday life.*

Praise the Lord, you do not have to figure this out on your own. Jesus knows exactly how you are doing. He knows your every struggle. He wants to be there for you. When you confess your weaknesses, God will be able to come and do what He does best, which is to restore you. Peter encourages you in 1 Peter 5:7 (NLT) to "Give all your worries and cares to God because He cares about you." When you give it all to God and tell Him of your needs, it is then you will be sustained and strengthened. The key here is opening your mouth and speaking out your needs. Some of you may not even know where to begin because you cannot articulate how you are feeling. All it takes at times is just sitting in God's presence and allowing His Holy Spirit to minister to you. While the Holy Spirit is ministering to you, He will reveal to you what is in your heart, and then you will be able to openly express to God and to others how you truly feel. I pray one day you will experience true transparent freedom.

So be encouraged, to be honest with your emotions. Do not allow fear to keep you from feeling life. If you are angry, depressed, feeling dissatisfied or discontent, say so. Own your emotions! Having strong emotions is natural. The key is learning how to express your emotions, without allowing them to overpower you. Tell Jesus how you are doing for He is here, and He is waiting to heal you. Besides, where else can you be your true and authentic self, if not in the presence of God? He wants all of you. Your heart and your emotions matter to Him.

PRAYER:

"Jesus, I thank you that I can be my real self with you. Please help me to always be transparent in your presence. Father, I declare that you are Lord over my soul. I align my emotions with your emotions so that they will no longer rule over me. Jesus, I pray you will become my emotional stability. Lord give me the courage to face any suppressed feelings. May you resurface them and give me wisdom on how to deal with it all. I lay my burdens at your feet. I pray that you will send the right counsel and good friends I can be myself with and share my heart with. You are the healer of my heart and the consolation of my soul. I want to be transparent with you, Jesus, for I know you can handle all of me. [Be encouraged right at this moment, to be transparent with the Lord and release your heart fully to Him. Afterward, spend some time in silence and ask the Father what He wants to say to you.]

I receive your peace and love. In Jesus' name, I pray, Amen."

Devotion 13: Growing Pains

"Growth is the only evidence of life." - John Henry Newman

Growing into the person God desires for you to become is never an easy process. Growth requires being stretched, tested, and most of all, being patient. For some of you, the mere mention of change and growth strikes fear into your heart. For a number of you, you feel as if your life has always been this way, and you have lost hope in things ever changing. Therefore, you have come to terms that things might just be better left untouched, so you won't be disappointed again. And for some of you, you disregard the possibility of change because life has turned out exactly as planned. So, what else could God do for you that He has not already done, or that you have not already done for yourself? Whether you are stricken with fear or whether you are satisfied with life, I believe God is calling you to a higher level in Him. You will have to make room for Christ to do a new work in you, in order for you to reach your highest potential. ***God is calling you to be more and He wants to give you bigger and this requires growth, and sometimes growing can be painful.***

God wants to expand your plans for your life. He wants to take you deeper, but will you go with Him? For some of you, the door for expansion has presented itself, but you have decided, that sort of risk would be too overwhelming and scary. ***Remaining where you are,***

has more severe consequences then adventuring into the domain of conquering the impossibilities of life. If you do not go then you will never know what you can become. What is impossible with man is possible with God. You cannot see the ending from the beginning. You can only see what today has to offer you. But what is good enough for you today may not be ample enough for you tomorrow. What God has for you is greater than what you have imagined for yourself.

Are you willing to go through the growing process God has for you, in order to birth forth the greatness that is within you? God will never require you to do anything that you are not capable of doing. He has set you up for success and not for failure. In order to be great for God and in God, you will have to make some sacrifices. For example, "What if being great in God means downsizing your home and money spending habits, for the salvation of thousands of souls?" "What if His greatness means leaving some of your personal dreams behind?" Sometimes, there will be hard decisions you will have to make in order for you to be prosperous according to God's will.

Enduring the growing pains of life is not only for your benefit but it is for the benefit of your family, your sphere of influence, and it is for the sake of nations that are waiting for you to reach your full potential in Christ. Your decision in choosing to grow will also impact the future generations to come. So be encouraged, for your growing pains will cause you to suffer, but only for a little while. "Your momentary, light distress [this passing trouble is producing for you an eternal weight of glory [a fullness] beyond all measure [surpassing all comparisons, a transcendent splendor and an endless blessedness" (2 Corinthians 4:17 AMP). After this temporary pain is done, you will give birth to new life. This new life will be worth every wound that turned into a scar, it is worth every time you had to push yourself beyond your capability, and every tear that was shed. Everything you have gained from growing in God, no one and nothing can take that away from you. **So, challenge yourself to grow in God, knowing that only the sky is your limit, but it is not His.**

<u>PRAYER:</u>

"Father, I pray that you will make my thinking like yours, so I can see and imagine all that you have for me. Sustain me during this growing process and give me the patience to wait on you. Stretch the areas of my life where you require me to do more. I want to go where you want me to go and do what you want me to do Jesus. I pray that my life decisions will positively impact future generations. I pray that you will bless all the work of my hands and cover them in your precious blood. Jesus, enlarge my territory and make your name great in my life. Thank you Lord, that this growing process is going to allow me to become the best version of myself. In Jesus' name, I pray, Amen."

Devotion 14: Well Isn't It Obvious

What man rejects God accepts. When they see rejection, God sees a master plan of divine redirection and a glorious transformation. – Laurine Voltaire

One of the greatest pains, I believe, we will ever have to endure is rejection. Rejection is one of the things that is often left unspoken about and disregarded. If you think about it, we all probably reject at least one person per month, and it can happen in a number of different ways. For example, how many times has someone opened the door for you and you did not acknowledge them by saying thank you? Instead, you just walk through the door like the wind blew it open for you. Or, how many times has someone smiled at you and you stare at them dead in the eye and do not smile back? How about when you are on your daily commute to work and you purposely scroll up your window when a homeless person tries to ask you for spare change? How would you feel if you were on the other side, needing help but no one was willing to hear your story? Maybe you have been the victim of rejection because of your skin color, socio-economic status, hair type, gender, or religion. We all know how it feels to be rejected and overlooked. ***Thankfully, we serve a God who will never reject us. God does not turn a blind eye to the needs of His people, because He sincerely loves them.*** God's perception of people is much different than ours. God does not focus on the outward appearance of a person, but He looks at the heart; for He knows we are weak and we are only made strong in Him.

In Mark chapter 10 verses 46-52, the Bible gives us the perfect illustration of how to totally break free from rejection. This story tells us about a blind man named Bartimaeus, who cried out to Jesus from among the crowd, because he hoped that Jesus would have mercy on him. At the beginning of the story, we find him begging by the roadside. Bartimaeus, I imagine was used to people stepping on him and passing him by without giving him a second thought. I can only wonder, how long blind Bartimaeus had been waiting for this moment to be seen. And now, He was going to have an encounter with Jesus.

The Bible story commences with Bartimaeus hearing a commotion of rushing footsteps ringing in his ears. This was the sound of Jesus, his disciples, and a large crowd leaving the city. This was Bartimaeus' big moment before Jesus left his hometown, and he made sure he was not going to miss out on his great opportunity to meet Jesus. So, he shouts two times from the top of his lungs, "Jesus, Son of David have mercy on me" (Mark 10:47 NKJV). In the midst of the noise and the chatter, Jesus hears the cry of this desperate man, and this stops Jesus in his tracks. Ironically, once Jesus sees Bartimaeus, he does not heal him right away. Instead, Jesus asks him Mark 10:51 (NKJV), "What do you want me to do for you?" Jesus clearly knows and sees that Bartimaeus cannot see. So why did Jesus ask him this question? Was not the answer obvious enough? Why didn't Jesus just use His healing power to heal Bartimaeus' eyes at that very moment? Most of you, if Jesus came into your situation and asked you a question that had an obvious answer to it, you would have been upset with Jesus. And, you probably would have reacted irrationally and prematurely.

I was perplexed after reading this passage, so I prayed to the Lord for clarity and the Lord said to me, ***It is not always the obvious thing that I desire for my people to be changed or healed from in their lives, Laurine.*** God sees beyond what we can see, and He goes deeper than human comprehension. I realized it is not always the things that are visible that need the greatest attention. Sometimes, what we perceive we need healing from is only surface based and God is concerned on getting to the deeper root of our heart issues, such as; rejection, anger, unforgiveness, depression, lust, loneliness, isolation, and despair. I also believe Jesus asked him this question because He wanted to find out what was Bartimaeus' expectation of Him. Jesus is a healer, a miracle worker, and Jesus is the Son of Man. But for Bartimaeus, ***Jesus is also the One who can extend mercy to a merciless people.*** I believe Bartimaeus wanted more than just the ability to see. He longed to be seen. He wanted to be affirmed that he was more than just a blind man by the wayside. He was a child of God. So, when he heard that powerful name of Jesus being shouted out on the streets, he felt the power behind that name and he was determined to get closer to Jesus.

You, just like Bartimaeus, are in close proximity to your healing. Jesus is near to you and He wants to surpass your expectation of Him. Right now, you may be feeling forgotten, overlooked, ignored, silenced, and pushed aside just like blind Bartimaeus. He was used to being told to be quiet in the midst of his pain and shame. But Bartimaeus was done being quiet. ***Are you done being silenced by your situation, as well?*** He was done living with this outward condition and with his inner torment. And because of Bartimaeus' faith, both sight and mercy were freely given to him. Mercy for his inner soul and sight to heal his outward being.

In my opinion, Bartimaeus did not believe Jesus was going to give him anything less than what he had asked Him for. Bartimaeus was blind, which means He could only have heard of the stories of Jesus healing the sick. He did not have to see any of the miracles Jesus performed, in order to believe that Jesus was more than capable to perform one for him.

Like Romans 10:17 (ESV) says, "Faith comes from hearing and hearing by the word of Christ." And the Word: Jesus Christ (John 1:1), called Bartimaeus to Himself and He made him whole.

What are you believing Jesus for today? Have you asked Him for it? And do you believe He is able to do it? Hebrews 11:6 (KJV) says, "Without faith, it is impossible to please God. You must believe that He will do it, and He is a rewarder of those who diligently seek Him." Therefore, put your trust in Jesus, for He is able to grant you the desires of your heart. Potentially, Jesus is desiring to give you something much deeper than what you are asking for. Either way, do not give up hope, for the Lord sees you. When you cry out to Him, you will get what your heart needs, and you will receive what your soul and spirit are yearning for.

So be encouraged, to give every hardened area of your heart to the Lord in great expectation that He is able to heal you from the inside and out. Call out to Jesus, for He is ready and willing to extend mercy to you. When you say the name of Jesus, you should not expect anything less than a wondrous work, for there is power in His name. Say it out loud and proud, "In Jesus' name, rejection shall not be my bitter drink or sour glass anymore." Your change is coming. Your change is here. Embrace it with arms opened wide, for nothing is too hard for your Lord. Just like He asked Bartimaeus, Jesus is asking you a question today and it is, "What can I do for you today, my child?" As you respond, be brave and release your heart to your Savior. Take a chance on Jesus and witness your brand-new miracle as it comes to life.

PRAYER:

"Lord, thank you for being Jehovah Jireh, the "One Who sees" everything that I go through. Thank you for the change you are bringing into my life. Father, help me to know that you are with me through it all and open my eyes to see that you have been standing, there right beside me all along. I desire to see the change you have for me, Lord, and I speak forth miracles, signs, and wonders to come into my life right now, in Jesus' name. I will no longer tolerate these bad conditions in my life. I will no longer be silenced by the naysayers, by my unbelief, or by the enemy. I will trust in the name of the Lord God Almighty to deliver me. Help me to believe your report for my life, for my expectation is only found in you. I am not rejected, but I am seen by Jesus and I am healed from every sickness and disease in the mighty name of Jesus. I love you, Lord. In Jesus' name, I pray, Amen."

Devotion 15: You Have A Life Worth Living

"Do not give up believing in God because He has not stopped believing in you. Great things are coming your way." – Laurine Voltaire

I read an article recently that broke my heart. It was about a pastor who passed away. He did not pass away from a sickly disease or from a tragic car accident, but from committing suicide. Dying from any of these other ways would have been just as horrible, but the fact that he died because he was struggling with a deep depression, that no one knew about, is what left me most heartbroken. It is really sad to say that this pastor is not the only pastor, leader, or may I dare say, Christian that has struggled with suicidal thoughts. Suicide is one of those issues, that is not really spoken about in the church. Some people do not think that Christians can be subjected to depressive thoughts that would lead them to the brink of wanting to take their own life. You would be surprised at the number of Christians who have prayed to God to die in their sleep or have begged Him, to take them to heaven, because the pains of life and the weight of it all, is too unbearable.

For most people, it is not as if, they do not realize they are being selfish by taking their own life. I am sure they know they will be terribly missed by their family and friends. I think people that commit or have attempted suicide have contemplated both of these factors and then some. Most people who suffer from suicidal thoughts believe suicide will take away their pain forever. Yes, it may take away your pain, but the pain that you are leaving behind just gets transferred into someone else's heart, the person(s) who must live without you. I am pretty sure your loved ones would rather have you be present in their life, instead of becoming a distant memory. ***You are too valuable, precious, and memorable to live without.***

As a devoted believer, I have suffered from suicidal thoughts a couple of times during my lifetime. In those moments, it did not matter how many encouraging words I had received, or what promises I knew God had in store for me. Nothing seemed to make me feel better. I would pray for myself, fast by myself, read the Bible to myself, and still, I was drowning in sorrow. Being by myself, alone, in isolation was the problem. In isolation, the devil tried his hardest to entangle me in his web of lies. He wanted me to think that there was no one in this world that could possibly understand what I was going through. ***What is the devil lying to you about today?*** If you do not silence him, eventually, your heart will believe these lies are truth, and these lies will slowly kill your hope, destroy your joy, and they will distort your image of God.

If you are wrestling with suicide, your battle is more than likely beyond your control. Your fight is not just against the negative thoughts that keep coming to your mind about your life, and it is not just about the trauma you have gone through or are enduring. Your struggle is also spiritual. The devil has come to entrap you with a spirit of heaviness and despair. I believe God is the ultimate Healer and He can set you free entirely. I also believe He has equipped doctors and medical professionals to help with the suicidal thoughts you are suffering from. Through these qualified individuals, you can get the attention that you need physically, emotionally, and mentally. However, when it comes to the spiritual side, it is God alone who is able to deliver you and set you free from the enemy.

This battle around and within you is not going to hinder the mighty plans God has over your life. ***You are going to come out of this.*** Believe me, when I say, ***God is not giving up on you so do not give up on yourself!*** It is by God's Word you will be set free. It is by God's power that you will be saved from ending your life. I know it does not seem like it now, but praising God even in the midst of your weakness, puts God above your hurts and it destroys the work of the enemy. Please know that you will need others to help you fight this, but right now, in this very moment, take action and do not give up hope! As you are sitting alone reading this devotion, begin to open your mouth and praise Jesus. If you do not know what to say, read some the psalms of praises out loud (Psalm 84-150). Then put on some worship music, dance in joy, and take your life back. If you cannot do it by yourself, call a friend to help you or visit a local Christian Bible-believing church and they will pray with you. ***You are never alone.***

By sharing your emotions with others, you will be delivered. ***The spiritual forces that are at work are only stronger and greater when you fight them alone, but they become much smaller and weaker when you fight them with others.*** I personally did not begin to come out of that dark place, until I let someone know I was struggling, tired, and ready to go home to heaven. You are not meant to do life alone. In Christ's strength and with the help of others, you will overcome this.

Recently I was able to minister to two broken women who wanted to end their lives because they felt like they failed as mothers. They were carrying a heavy load of guilt and self-condemnation; a load that was never the Lord's plan for His daughters to bear. With the help of the Holy Spirit and a friend, we were able to minister to these women by encouraging them to express their inner hurts to their heavenly Father. Freedom broke loose in that room the moment they both heard God speak hope into their dead situations. They felt the Father's love wiping away all their shame. I believe today, once you express your brokenness to the Father, you will also witness that there is freedom from the spirit of suicide, in Jesus' name.

So be encouraged, for even when everything around you is saying, "Give up" and "It's not worth it", Hope will whisper "Try again". Peace will shout out, "Will you be mine?" While Jesus is proclaiming, "I died so that you do not have to". Accept Christ's invitation to live. Now, all that is left for you to say is, "Help me".

Choose Life, my friend, for there is a reason why Life has chosen you.

<u>PRAYER:</u>

"Father God, I know you have a great plan for my life. Forgive me for my sins and I confess my faults before you now. Help me to know I am forgiven. Jesus, help me to fight these suicidal thoughts. I cannot do this by myself anymore. I pray for you to intervene in my life and to remove everything that has come to cause division and death with your purpose for my life. Spirit of death, I rebuke you, in Jesus' name. Spirit of suicide, grief, depression, condemnation, and heaviness, I rebuke you, in Jesus' name. Every evil spirit that has come to attack me, I rebuke you, in Jesus' name. Leave my life! I remove your authority over my emotions, my mind, heart, and life in Jesus' name. I bind your power over me here on earth as you are already bound in heaven and I rebuke all of these evil spirits to the place of no return in Jesus' name. I uproot all the lies of the devil in my heart and I renounce and break their power over me in Jesus' name. I receive your Word as truth Lord, and your truth is I am free.

I release God's peace, joy, happiness, and contentment over me. Jesus, you control my inner and outer being. Restore my hope for living each day. Jesus, I want to see you face to face. You are my light in the midst of darkness and you are my joy in the midst of agony. You are my hope to live a life without the memory of pain. I have a life worth living in you. Grant me the serenity to see there is more to life than what I have been living. Give me the strength to seek help and please send the right people down my path to give me wise counsel.

I pray for all the families that have lost someone to suicide. I pray you will give them peace and your love to comfort them through this trying time. I pray you will give courage to those who are suffering to speak out and ask for help. Jesus, you are my hiding place, my security, and I want you to become my everything. In Jesus' name, I pray, Amen."

Devotion 16: I Won't Accuse You

God pardons like a mother, who kisses the offense into everlasting forgiveness. – Henry Ward Beecher

Have you ever disobeyed your mother and touched the fire when she told you not to? When that happened, the first person that you immediately cried for was your mother, right? Even though you knew you would be grounded for the rest of your life, she was still the one you turned to for help. Most likely, you called your mother for help because since she is the one who told you not to do it, she more than likely also knows how to make you feel better. Once your mother heard your cry, she came running like the superhero she is, to nurse and to take care of your wound. And to your surprise, instead of yelling at you and punishing you, she bandaged it up, and she kissed it. Why didn't she yell at you? Any good parent knows that the pain from the wound sometimes, is the greatest lesson, so there is no need to reprimand the sin. You will never forget how much it hurts because the wound will almost always leave a scar. Even more so, I believe, that you will never forget the grace and forgiveness you received from your parent after you disobeyed them. Therefore, you will be more inclined to resist the next temptation, and the likelihood of you repeating the same mistake is less probable.

This is what God does with you. He does not have to repeatedly remind you of your past offenses toward Him. He knows that the sting from your past experiences will sometimes leave you so scarred to the point, you will be more than willing, to obey His word the next time around. ***When you choose to learn the lessons behind the "No's" of God, you will come to a new understanding and reverence for His presence. He is not doing it to shame or disappoint you, but He is saying "No" to protect you from what you cannot see. God does not want you to become a repeat offender of the sins, that He died for you to be victorious over.***

This imagery of God's love being a protective shield over us, reminds me of one of my favorite Bible stories found in John 8:1-11 titled: *The Adulterous Woman.* In this story the scribes and Pharisees brought a woman to Jesus and were accusing her of adultery. I believe many of them probably only heard from a third party of what she had done, nevertheless, they were condemning her like they caught her red-handed. They stood as onlookers judging her life, barely understanding how she got to that very point in the first place. There was a seed that caused her to commit adultery which could have come from insecurity, loneliness, or pride. Who knows! I am not condoning her behavior at all, sin is sin. However, when we do not know someone's story, we should take the time to get to know them, so we can iron out all the details before-hand, to help them from stumbling again instead of judging them. I believe, since the scribes and Pharisees were the spiritual leaders in that time, they should have picked her up and showed her mercy, instead of mocking her in front of everyone. It is likely they ridiculed her in front of the entire town to see Jesus' reaction. They figured that if Jesus did not accuse her, then He condones sin, but if He does condemn her then He is just like them. What these leaders failed to understand was that Jesus is love, so He would never have taken that opportunity to teach a lesson out of her life. Being humiliated was enough of a lesson for this adulterous woman. Graciously, Jesus did not retaliate by fighting fire with fire at the expense of this woman's life, to help endorse this mockery. Jesus took the high road and used a profound statement to stop everyone in their tracks. Jesus said in John 8:7

(ESV), "Let him who is without sin among you be the first to throw a stone at her." Well obviously, everyone there must have committed a sin or two in their lives because none of them were able to uphold Jesus' request. But hold on, "Was not Jesus without sin?" Jesus had every right to stone this adulterous woman. "So why did Jesus not cast the first stone?"

Jesus did not come to cast stones or to beat people down. Jesus came to become the cornerstone in which you and I can rest, lean, and stand firm on. Jesus did not come to condemn this adulterous woman. Jesus wanted the adulterous woman to leave that place standing on her own two feet healed, made whole, and leaning on Him as her solid rock. He did not have to throw a rock to prove His righteousness to any of the religious leaders because He is God, and God never has to prove His ways to anyone. Jesus, as well as everyone else there, knew, that this adulterous woman felt guilty about what she had done. I can just imagine her weeping hysterically as she is thinking that these are her final moments here on earth, and all that is going to be remembered of her is that she was an adulterer. But Jesus made sure that this would not be the case for her. He decided to love on her instead, and this showed the religious leaders that love is the only way to clean up anyone's mess from their past. This is how you and I are to behave. We should always love people in spite of the sins they have committed. When we choose to walk in love, we will see everyone through the eyes of our Creator. Therefore, instead of judging people, we should pray for them to be set free. Jesus will never throw stones at you or throw the bad things you have done in your past, back in your face as a form of retaliation, revenge, or as spitefulness. People do enough of that and so can life.

So be encouraged today and do not become discouraged, if you are surrounded by people who are judging you for what you have done in the past. And do not be afraid if they are ready to cast stones and ruin your reputation. Jesus is your mighty vindicator and He will show up for you by silencing your enemies. If you have been struggling with sin, all Jesus wants is for you to confess your wrongdoings and to pray a prayer of repentance (which is asking for a change of heart), so that you can start living your best life now. Jesus has not come to accuse you, but God sent Jesus to save you from your sins. In John 3:17 (ESV) the Bible says, "Jesus did not come into the world to condemn the world but in order that the world might be saved through Him." ***Jesus came to help you out of your mess to turn your life into a powerful message.*** After He picks you up, make sure you pay it forward by encouraging another brother or sister in need. If you are like one of those religious leaders, clenching onto a stone in your hand, you might want to think twice before throwing it against someone who has sinned against you or your loved one. I pray God will give you the grace to release every offense and judgment from your heart. There is only one Judge, and the same Judge who forgave you has forgiven them as well. Through the power of His loving-kindness, you will be able to forgive yourself and your offenders.

PRAYER:

"Father, thank you for your love that sees past my sins, and that does not condemn me but saves and delivers me. Thank you, Jesus, for not allowing me to die in my sins. David says in Psalm 40:2 (ESV), "You upheld my feet from the miry clay and you set my feet upon a rock." I pray I will always walk on leveled ground in wholeness and holiness with you, Lord. Give me the grace to forgive others who have wronged me publicly or in secret. Give me the grace to forgive others when they have sinned publicly or privately against me, my loved ones, or your church. Help me to see the need to pray for them and not to accuse them. Lord, please help those who are hiding now, those who need your grace to come out of darkness, so that they may also walk in your light of truth. Help me to stand and speak up for the injustices that I see around me. May your truth light my path and may I always seek your wisdom to be my daily guide. In Jesus' name, I pray, Amen."

Devotion 17: Receiving Forgiveness

"As far as the east is from the west so far has, He removed our transgressions from us." - Psalm 103:12 (NIV)

It is not always the easiest thing to receive forgiveness from others and especially from an Almighty God, when deep down inside you know, you are guilty. This weight of condemnation will blind and block you from receiving the love that God is so willing and eager to give you. As far as the highest heaven is from the lowest pit on the earth, so is the length of God's love for you. ***His love is as deep as the sharpest nails that have pierced the hands and the feet of Jesus. This is the magnitude, the measure, and the extremity God has taken to demonstrate His love for you. He wants to reassure you that ALL of your past sins have been paid for in full and you have been forgiven.***

If God can so easily forgive and forget our sins, then why is it so difficult for us to forget our wrongdoings? I think it is because our past has the ability to haunt us like a reoccurring ghost, peek-a-booing in and out of our lives whenever it pleases. The enemy, who is also known as the accuser of the brethren, will try to use our past sins as evidence against us, in hopes, that we will be found guilty before the judgment of God. But praise the Lord, the blood of Jesus speaks louder than the accusations of Satan. Jesus' blood has paid the price for your sins and you will be found not guilty. The Bible says in Isaiah 54:17 (NIV), "No weapon forged against you will prevail, and you will refute every tongue that accuses." God has given you the authority to be victorious over your past.

Whatever decisions you have made in the past, it is your responsibility to own up to it, to confess your faults before God and to your accountability partners, so that you may be healed. I know it is easier said than done, mainly because of the society we live in. It is hard to share your weakness and struggles with others without the consequence of being judged or feeling condemned. So, of course, you would much rather keep to yourself and remain in isolation, even though inwardly, you are perishing. And for some of you, you are just too afraid to deal with what you have done. You do all you can to hide the darkest secrets of your past, thus making sure not even the greatest detective is able to find the skeletons that are hiding in your closet. How many of you know that even if you have worked all of your life to hide the darkest secrets of your past, they will *ALL eventually* come to light? For the Bible says in Luke 8:17 (NIV), "There is nothing hidden that will not be disclosed." Ephesians 5:12 (ESV) says, "For it is shameful even to speak of the things that are done by them in secret." Your past secrets can make you feel so shameful of the acts you have committed. Some of you hold yourself in deep contempt for the choices that you have made, and an immense sense of regret indefinitely overpowers you.

Your past mistakes are no longer yours to bear and you do not have to live in fear of being judged. God is not going to let anyone throw your past in your face or hold it as leverage over your life. God has given you His Spirit of power to let go of your past, calmness to know you are forgiven, and a well-balanced mind to walk in His forgiveness. Sooner or later, you are going to have to face your past head-on. Your past has controlled your future and has dictated your decisions long enough, and it is time to take back control over your life. God wants you to bring your past sins to Him so that you can review the situation together. Not to re-live what has happened or to re-traumatize you of your past circumstances, but He wants to get to the root of it all so that it never happens again. I believe God wants you to reveal the hidden hurts of your heart to Him, in full disclosure, not withholding any details or emotional expressions. This is the first step to moving forward.

So be encouraged, to be bold and tell God of all your fears, lay your shame down at His feet, and receive His forgiveness. Your freedom and healing will come directly from the Lord. It will also come from the safety of being a part of a community that is able to walk alongside you through your process of restoration (James 5:16). You should always ask God for wisdom as to who you should share your life experiences with, because He has already given those people grace and love, to carry your burdens to the cross with you. My spiritual parents always say, "We learn in isolation, but we are healed in community." God is in the story writing business and He is ready to start a new chapter in your life, if you will allow Him to. He will use your entire life's story for His glory and He will create a redemptive novel out of it. What do you think the Bible is? It is comprised of stories, about broken people who have been redeemed by a loving God. After you let it all go, God will show you that He has been patiently waiting on you all along. God longs to exchange your pain for His love, your shame for His freedom, and your burdens for His peace. Sometimes, this process will have to be daily, but every day, by you choosing to move forward in Christ, you will become a better and newer you.

<u>PRAYER:</u>

"Jesus, I receive your forgiveness today. Thank you, Lord, that my past sins have been forgiven because of the cross. Help me to release all those I have blamed, including myself. Father let every hidden transgression, every evil intent in my life and in my heart be made known and expose it, in Jesus' name. Rid my life of all shame, blame, and unwillingness to forgive. By your power, I cast it away forever, in Jesus' name. May your light penetrate every dark place, leaving no hold of Satan over me. Please, purify me and remove the influences of my past iniquities over my flesh. Free me from all addictions, bondages, and strongholds, Lord. I declare I am a holy child of God and I am victorious. My past no longer defines my identity. Only your words of truth and what You have spoken over me gives me life and substance. Your words fuel my desire to keep living."

[Begin to pray and to speak over your life what you hear and know God has called you to be: free, whole, more than a conqueror, favored, etc.]

"I receive your peace and love in my heart. Jesus, I pray that you send the right people my way, those who are willing to walk alongside me and who will help me in my brokenness. Give me the strength to share my story with others to encourage them as I have been encouraged. I have been set free by Jesus and I am truly free, indeed. I declare I will live in your freedom every day of my life, in Jesus' name, I pray, Amen."

Devotion 18: Hand in Hand: True Friendship is a Beautiful Thang

"A friend is really like a long-lost family member you find throughout time and you love them as if you shared the same womb." - Laurine Voltaire

My mom always told me, "If someone shows you who they are the first time, believe them." Another one of her phrases I loved was, "If you fool me once, shame on you and if you fool me twice, shame on me." In life, you only need a handful of close friends. It is better to count them on one hand than to count them on two. In the Bible, we read that Jesus had 12 disciples that followed Him everywhere He went, learning the secrets of the kingdom of God. In Matthew chapter 18, however, Jesus only invited three of these disciples, Peter, John, and James up the mountain and He revealed Himself to them in a new way. Also, in Matthew 26:36-38 in the Garden of Gethsemane, Jesus told these same three to sit and to pray because His soul was in anguish. I believe He chose these three deliberately. Peter, John, and James were able to see Jesus' kingly and divine self on top of the mountain, and they were able to see His human and weak-side that was desperately crying out for help, in the garden.

I believe the lesson Jesus was trying to teach us about friendship, is that not everyone is able to handle your true self. You will have some friends like the 12 disciples, who will support you in most areas of your life and they will sincerely desire for you to excel in Christ. Then out of that bigger group of friends, I believe you will have a handful of them, who God has hand-picked to love and to carefully handle both your spiritual-side and your human-side. These are the type of friends who value the anointing and the call of God upon your life. But at the same time, they know that you are still human, and you will need their help from time to time. You need these kinds of friends. We all need these kinds of friends.

You should desire friends that are going to propel you to the next place that God has for you. Your friends should see you as a new creation and they should not judge you for your former mistakes. You need friends that will place you above themselves and friends that will rejoice when you are successful, and they will pray for you when you are weak. Friends that are going to walk with you and not on you. Pray for God to give you friends that are going to laugh with you and not behind your back. True friends that will alleviate your burdens and not be the cause of them. And you need real friends, who will not walk away from you when you make a mistake, but they will stand by you even when everybody else is ashamed of you.

So be encouraged, for if you have friends that encourage, motivate, and support you, then you are blessed. If you do not, you are just one prayer away from receiving life-long journey partners, that will be with you through thick and thin. If you do not know if your current friends are good for you, just measure your friends against the best friend you will ever have: Jesus. ***No one will ever be as perfect or as cool as Jesus, but you know you have a really good friend to hold your hand if he or she is striving to be just like Him.*** I have always found that a good friend is a person who will laugh at your jokes even when they are not funny, pray you through your hurts when the pain is too much, and offer a clean sleeve and a strong shoulder to lean on when you feel like giving up. Most importantly, a good friend encourages you, to draw nearer to Christ to become the best you can be. Surely, a good friend is a gift from God.

<u>PRAYER:</u>

"Father, I pray that you will send me the right friends in my life. Friends that display a godly character and friends that live for you. I pray for the friends that I have now, that you will bless them. Lord, teach me how to be a good friend. Let all of my friendships grow in godly love and peace. Lord please take away any friends that are not good for me. Thank you, Jesus, for being my closest friend, sweetest companion, and the One who loves me for all I am. Father, may I befriend those who do not feel worthy of love, sharing with them the same unconditional love you have given me. In Jesus's name, I pray, Amen."

Devotion 19: Let God Off the Hook (BLAME)

"Many of our troubles occur because we base our choices on unreliable authorities; culture ("everyone is doing it"), tradition ("we've always done it"), reason ("it seems logical"), or emotion ("it just felt right")." - Rick Warren

I am sure, while you were growing up as a child, your parents would give you strict instructions about the rules you had to abide by. For example, your parents would tell you not to cross the street without an adult because you will get hit by a car. As a kid though, you somehow convince yourself that you are invincible, and you believe that nothing can possibly hurt you. So even though you heard those instructions from your parents, you still attempted to get the ball, that you kicked in the middle of the street. And as a result, your mom or dad had to grab you before you got hit by a car. As you get older, this pattern of rebellion does not go away. It begins to intensify the moment you realize you are an adult, and now you have the freedom to make your own decisions. It is called free-will. The problem with having free-will is that, if you do not make the right choice the first time, there is no reversing the effects of your decision. Unless God intervenes.

In Proverbs 19:3 (NLT & AMP), the Bible says, "A person

ruins their lives by their own foolishness (NLT); then his heart is resentful and rages against the Lord [for, being a fool, he blames the Lord instead of himself]" (AMP). There is an ownership and a responsibility that needs to be taken if a person chooses to go their own way instead of God's way. We should always rely on the concrete and unchanging counsel that comes from the Word of God, instead of allowing ourselves to be influenced by others or by our own emotions.

God is holy and He does not endorse, nor influence our bad decision making. There are no little white lies or acceptable sins in the kingdom of heaven. In James 1:13 (NIV) the Bible says, "When tempted, no one should say, "God is tempting me." For God cannot be tempted by evil, nor does he tempt anyone." God is always the first one to tell you to resist temptation and to resist the devil, so he can flee from you (James 4:7). But, because you and I are stubborn, we end up falling into sin, even though God sends many roadblocks, signs, and people our way to divert us from it. When a stubborn or rebellious person's mind and heart is made up, and they are fixated on doing the wrong thing, it is hard to convince them of the right path. So, when all is said and done, and after their decisions have left them in a broken mess, they tend to blame God for their tears and for their pain.

Why? Well, the common belief among many people is that, if God did not want all of this bad stuff to happen, then He would have stopped it from happening in the first place. On the contrary, I believe God does try to stop us from falling into sin and into the traps of the enemy. In Genesis 2:17, God warned Adam and Eve not to eat any fruit from the tree of knowledge of good and evil, but they did it anyway. As for you and I, God has given us His Holy Spirit who grants us discernment between right and wrong, and He is able to keep us from stumbling. It is the sin that lives in our hearts that causes us to fall, not God. The way I see it is like this: we need to stop compromising our moral and spiritual integrity to fleshly and worldly pleasures, and we need to start contending in the spirit for what we believe in.

Let's be real, do you really think that a loving God, who gave His only Son for us, would want us to suffer here on this earth? The very place He gave as our inheritance? No! There will be many trials and tests that will come our way, but God will give us the grace to overcome them all. When bad things happen to us, we should not blame God. But we need to seek the meaning behind these trials. Sometimes these trials come, because God is trying to work some things out of our lives like: bad habits or temperaments. Or, sometimes these trials are about building our character to make us more like Jesus Christ. At the end of the day, trials are never easy to go through, and I know you have probably been through several circumstances that have been out of your control. Instead of blaming God for these setbacks, I would encourage you to ask God questions in prayer; to hear His truth. When you do so, most assuredly God will give you the rest you need for your soul.

Most times, the way our lives turn out is determined by the choices we make, and by how submitted or reluctant we are to the perfect will of the Lord. I love this anonymous quote that says, **"Some people create their own storms, then get upset when it rains."** When God says "No" and we rebuttal with a "Yes" we should not get upset when it begins to rain on our parade. For example, you may have said "Yes" to that relationship when God said "No" and now you are heartbroken. You said "Yes" to those extra late-night fast food meals when God and the doctors said "No" and now you have high cholesterol and blood pressure. You said "Yes" to watching pornography when God said "No", and now the spirit of perversion has invaded your home, and you wonder why your children are sexually active, and why your marriage is broken. You said "Yes" to those late night after work dinners with your coworker and now you have found yourself in adultery. And you said "Yes" to having one last cigarette just to find out, now you have cancer. No matter what mistakes you have made in the past and no matter the mistakes you will make today and tomorrow, it is never too late to turn away from your foolishness. Learn the important lessons from your downfall. So, the next time temptation comes knocking at your door, determine within yourself that you will not have a conversation with the enemy. But the next time he comes creeping around, you will slam the door in his face and you will rise up and do what is right.

What I love about God is that even though He knows we are to blame for the sins we have committed, He does not point and wag His index finger at us saying, "You should have known better." Instead, He opened His hands and extended His palms, so that they could be pierced for our sins. And then, with those same hands, He reaches down low, scoops us up, and He saves us from our messy lives. God is love and His reason for loving us is determined by His character. God's love for you is not influenced by who you are, what you have done, or by what you can do. So be encouraged, for if you choose to stop playing the blame game with God, and instead, you choose to admit and confess your faults, you will surely be forgiven. Do not allow your past wrongs or offenses, to be replayed in your mind day after day. Let God off the hook and let yourself off the hook, too. At the end of it all, it is much easier to blame God, but it is more freeing to just be healed by Him. Choose healing over blame and you will never be the same.

<u>PRAYER:</u>

"Father, forgive me for every time I have blamed you when it was not your fault. I confess my sins before you. God, help me not to compare my failed experiences to your love for me. Your love is unchanging. Make right the wrong decisions and choices I have made. Create in me a clean heart and renew in me a steadfast spirit willing to obey. God, help me to know that you love me in spite of what I have done or what has been done to me. Just because people have failed me and I have failed myself does not mean that you, Lord, will do the same to me. Help me to forgive myself. I release the anger I have in my heart towards you Lord and I place the weight and the burden of my blame in your hands. I sentence, blaming you to death and I declare your restoring life reigns in me. In Jesus' name, I pray, Amen."

PART 3.

Joy In Waiting:

God's Timing Is Perfect

Devotion 20: Lord, Please Give Me a Sign!

"Thus, says the Lord, stand by the roads, and look, and ask for the ancient paths where the good way is; and walk in it, and find rest for your souls." - Jeremiah 6:16 (ESV)

Have you ever felt like your life is similar to a never-ending dream? I often imagine that one day I will eventually wake up to my real life, the one I think I should be living. A life without suffering, sorrow, regrets, disappointments, and worries. If you are like me, you may have imagined your life going in a completely different direction than it is today. And for a hand full of you, your life may seem like a movie, which would be cool, only if you were the leading lady or man. But instead of being the hot throb, you may feel more like an onlooker, the understudy, or an extra. It is as if you are simply just watching life as it passes you by. Lastly, some of you may be feeling like you have no control over what is going on in your life right now. You may even be feeling absolutely numb and lost. You may feel like your life is being lived without you experiencing it. Do I have any witnesses?

If you have ever been in this place, like I have, you may be in desperate need of knowing what in the world is going on. You are in need of a sign. I am talking about having the Creator and living

God speaking directly into your situation. For most of us, when we eagerly desire for God to speak into our situation, we envision the heavens opening up and then we will see, written in bold letters, "Here is your sign, my child!" Unfortunately, the likelihood of the heavens parting on our behalf is slim to none. Although God may not always speak the way we may want Him to, He is capable of doing something greater than we can ever anticipate. Throughout the Bible, when the people needed a sign, God would send His power, His glory, and His angels as encouragement and as a reminder, that His presence would never abandon them. If you need guidance in this hour, God is here, and He will never lean a deaf ear towards your cry for help. In Isaiah 65:24 (NIV), God says these soothing words to His people, "Before they call I will answer; while they are still speaking, I will hear." God is ready and willing to show you His glory.

Realistically, waiting for God to give you a sign can be tiring. Once in a while, you can feel divided on the inside. For example, your mind may be pondering the motives of God in making you wait for Him, while your soul may be battling doubt and confusion, trying its best to hold onto hope. Although you may feel understandably lost, you have to remember, God is in control of your life and He will never let you down. He will give you clues or signs to this puzzling journey along the way, that you must pay close attention to. These signs are not always going to be practical and obvious. If you pray for your spiritual eyes to open, you will inevitably see them. These signs will lead you into the perfect destiny God has already set out for you.

Here are some examples of different signs, places, and seasons, you may be currently facing, in your faith walk with the Lord. Remember, wherever there is a sign from the Lord in your life, there is a specific word He is speaking over you to empower you, and there are lessons to be learned to mature you.

SIGN # 1: The Valley

Right now, you are feeling like you are walking through the valley. Which is a sign, and not a good one, because valleys represent a low place, a place of darkness, and death. David and Ezekiel both found themselves in valleys. Valley experiences, though dark, do not have to stay that way. David said in Psalm 23 that even though he walked through the valley, he would not fear, because he knew that God was with him. What we can learn from David's experience is that ***you are only meant to walk through valleys. You are not meant to camp in them***.

Ezekiel also found himself in a valley, a valley of dry bones, where everything was lifeless and helpless. God taught Ezekiel that even in the valley, when it seems like there is no way out, ***you can speak to your situation and see those dry places come to life.*** The same goes for you. You can speak to those dry bones in your life and watch as they come back alive. The valley experience is not meant to kill you, but to mature you. As you are walking through it, you will gain more confidence in God. Also, you will walk in hope knowing the Lord is with you on every side, so there is no need to fear anything that comes your way.

Sign # 2: The Wilderness

Sometimes you will find yourself in the wilderness, feeling like nothing on this earth can quench your thirst. Nothing seems to be working as it should. You have dibbled and dabbled in just about everything, looking for pleasure, but still, you are left hungry and unsatisfied. Your old methods and lifestyle are not satisfactory any more. This is the place the people of Israel found themselves in for 40 years because God was testing their hearts. God wanted them to cross over into the Promised Land, but He needed to show them their hearts beforehand. God does not desire to have second place in your heart and life. In this dry season, God is trying to get your attention. He is removing idols, past hurts, and regrets from your heart. The lesson learned in this season is that ***God is the only One that can satisfy you in every way because He is able to provide for your needs.***

SIGN # 3: Imprisonment

Right now, you are feeling like you are in prison and you need a sign of how you are going to get out. In Genesis chapters 39-40, we read the story of Joseph, who was sent to prison after being falsely accused of trying to commit adultery with Potiphar's wife. It seemed like Joseph just could not get a break. First, his brothers threw him into the pit. Next, he was sold into slavery. Then, just when things were getting better, while he was in Potiphar's house, he was accused of hitting on his master's wife. Though innocent, he was still placed in chains. Although Joseph was forgotten by man, he was never forgotten by God. God did not leave Joseph in prison and He is not planning on leaving you in yours. You are coming out of this, on top and in charge. I encourage you to take on the mindset of Paul and Silas in Acts 16:16-40 and ***praise your way out that prison.*** Praise your way out of those chains, addictions, and strongholds and they will all be broken off, in Jesus' name.

SIGN # 4: Hiding Out

Right now, you are in a place of isolation and hiding, where you do not want to speak to anyone, not even God. You want to be left alone. No matter how much you want to push God away, He will find you and take care of your needs because God will not allow you to die in isolation. Elijah, in 1 Kings 19, ran away to Mount Horeb because he was scared, he was going to be killed. Even in the midst of being fearful, bewildered, and questioning the voice of God, God provided for Elijah and met him where he was. Just like Elijah, you may have run away from God, church, or from your family, hoping to stay alone in isolation forever because the pain is too much to bear.

You are too afraid to face your fears. You will learn in this place, that ***you are not meant to be brave on your own. God is able to give you strength and boldness to make it through. The only place you are meant to hide in is in the secret place of the Most High, where you will find rest with God.***

SIGN # 5: Change

Every once in a while, you will find yourself in a place where everything and everyone around you has changed. Change will come in all different shapes, sizes, and circumstances. Your inner circle may change. Your relationship status may change. The size of your family may change. Your job may change. Your desires may change and so on. Change is not always the easiest thing for us to deal with but there comes a point in time when we must learn to ride the waves of change that come our way, instead of allowing them to continue to crash over us. In John chapter 15, the Bible says that you are the branch attached to the vine, who is Jesus, and He will help you to produce healthy things in your life. The Vinedresser, who is God, will cut off all loose ends in your life. In this place, you will learn that ***change does not always have to be a bad thing. Sometimes, it is necessary in order for God to get you to the place, you need to be.***

Pastor and author Max Lucado uses a brilliant statement to sum up our faith walk with God. He states: "God never said that the journey would be easy, but He did say that the arrival would be worthwhile." Therefore, take these signs as an opportunity to endeavor on a worthwhile adventure with Jesus, as He leads you into your Promised Land. During your times of prayer, ask the Lord to help you recall to mind the signs He has been showing you along the way. Then, match up these signs, with scriptures from the Bible and with different Bible stories. By doing this, you will see that God is trying to teach you precious life principles and He is leading you on His path of righteousness or right living. I believe God is preparing you for your next level of greatness. You will by God's grace and favor finish the race you have begun. So be encouraged, and have full confidence in this, what God has begun in your life, He is committed to fully accomplishing it.

PRAYER:

"Father, thank you for the signs you have shown me along the way. Thank you for your signs of protection and your signs of grace and mercy towards me. Thank you for your signs of provision and tender love. Lord, please allow my heart to know that in every season I find myself in, you will always be there with me. Lord, I am trusting you to lead me to my Promised Land. I pray my heart and soul will be still before you no matter what season I find myself in. Please reveal your Word to me in a new way, for I want to see my story in your Word. I desire to hold fast to your promises and to your blessings for me, according to thy Word. The Bible says in Psalm 119:105 (ESV), "Your word is a lamp unto my feet and a light unto my path." Father illuminate your Holy Scriptures into my heart, so I may know you better. Thank you Holy Spirit, for always being the sign Jesus has sent for me, to feel the Father's tangible presence here on earth. All this I pray, in the beautiful name of Jesus Christ, Amen."

Devotion 21: Having Faith in the Unknown

"We gain strength, and courage, and confidence, by each experience in which we really stop to look fear in the face...we must do that which we think we cannot." Eleanor Roosevelt

When we do what we think we cannot, we begin to operate in the realm of supernatural faith. Only through Christ are we able to find faith in the most despised, unlikely, and unimaginable places. There are countless people of great faith found in the Bible, who despite their challenges, faced fear head on. I believe these heroes of faith were all secured that God's love would never fail them, and His love would triumph over all their uncertainties of life. They walked in courageous faith because they knew, firsthand, that the perfect love of God drives and expels all fear.

What challenges are you facing today, that are trying to shake your faith, bring you down, and make you doubt God's ability to see you through? You must get to a point in your life where you determine within yourself, that even in the most unreasonable times and conditions, you will stand firm no matter what, trusting in your God just like these heroes and pillars of faith did. It is not easy, but it is possible.

Let us briefly explore some of the lives of these heroes found in the Old Testament. In Daniel chapter 3, Shadrach, Meshach, and Abednego found faith in exile, in Babylon, in the midst of pagan worshippers and foreign gods. Even though the Babylonians kicked God out their country by refusing to worship Him, they could not kick God out of the hearts of these three Hebrew boys, despite the king's decree. Refusing to bow down to the image of king Nebuchadnezzar almost cost them their lives. But still, they trusted in God and they mustered up the strength to say no to compromise and yes to being totally sold out for Yahweh. At the end of their moral stand, the Son of Man met the boys in the fire and they marched out in victory. In the book of Genesis, from chapters 12 to chapter 21, here we find, the unfolding story of Abraham who found faith in the most unthinkable circumstance. His wife Sarah was barren, and God promised them that they were going to have a child from her very barren womb, and that Abraham would be the father of many nations. And after waiting for about 25 years, at the age of 100 years old, God's promise to Abraham came to pass, and he had a healthy baby boy named Isaac.

In 1 Samuel chapter 17, David had great faith to take five smooth stones to defeat the giant Goliath, who was taunting the armies of Israel. None of the older men or the great warriors before him, not even the king of Israel, was brave enough to go against this giant. Nevertheless, through David's faith, he was able to kill Goliath and restore the integrity of the nation. In Esther chapter 3, Esther's faith in God is greatly demonstrated, as she went unsummoned before the king to prevent the genocide of her nation. She knew going before the king could put her life in jeopardy. But yet, she was still willing to stand in the gap, and God favored her, and the people's lives were spared.

One example of a person of faith, that is seen in the New Testament, is the life of none other than, the apostle Paul. This man was beaten with rods, shipwrecked three times, put in prison, he was stoned, and left for dead; all for the sake of preaching the gospel (2 Cor. 11:25, Acts 14:9). And yet, Paul never lost hope in God. He continued to write letters of encouragement to the churches, from a prison cell, telling them to have faith in Jesus at all times. I could go on and on about the countless people of faith like: Noah, Gideon, Joshua, Peter, and John, who took a chance to trust in the Lord. In the end, they all witnessed that the Lord was greater than the tribulation that was before them.

These heroic Bible figures chose to serve the Lord by faith, even when they did not know what the outcome would be. Most importantly, they put their lives in harm's way to show that they were not ashamed to put their faith in their God. Now, Jesus is not asking for you to die for Him, but He is calling you, as God's child, to step it up a couple of notches in your faith game. *You need to take your faith to the next level! You must take risks in doing what you normally would not do, to make way for what you normally would not see.* This requires you to be bold enough to take God at His word and to go beyond your comfort zone.

So, with that being said, in what area of your life does God want to increase your faith? God may be asking you to do things that seem a bit scary right now, and it may not even make that much sense. But through experience, you will learn to trust Him. *God will never place you in a situation to cause you to fail. He will only take you into a place where He knows you will succeed and make it through. You will never know if you have faith unless you are put in a predicament where faith is needed.* So be encouraged, to start building and strengthening your faith muscles by praying, reading the Bible, and by being obedient to what God is asking you to do. For some of you, you may need to change your surroundings and start partnering with other believers: who are ready to cash in all of their chips and place their bet on having faith in Jesus. Putting all your hope in Jesus, will guarantee you a gracious and prosperous return. Step out in faith for it is time to start seeing and making your dreams come true. If you can imagine God doing great things for you in your mind and believe it with your heart, eventually, this will become the reality of your life, but only through your faith. The righteous walk by faith, talk by faith, and live by faith, so when needed, they will have courageous faith in the unknown.

<u>PRAYER:</u>

"Father, teach me to walk in your faith all the days I am here on earth. Restore my faith in you, Lord. Where it has been diminished, may my faith in you increase and your faith in me increase. God, open my eyes to see the things that I have been blinded to. Open my ears to hear the things that I have been deaf to. Open my mouth to speak to the mountains in my life that I have been afraid of. Your faith lives and resides in me through your promised Holy Spirit. God, grant me the grace to walk faithfully in your ways. Grant me the courage, to be unashamed about my faith and unashamed about the gospel, for it is the power of God unto salvation for all those who believe. Blanket me in your love, as I step out into the unchartered territory you have called me to conquer. Lead me, Lord, on your path of righteousness and help me to believe there are no limitations in you and there are no barriers that can hold me back. Empower me with your strength, to destroy all of the giants that stand before me. Show me your glory, and may your name be glorified in my life so that others will fear your great name. In Jesus' name, I pray, Amen."

Devotion 22: The Hardships of Being Single in a Modern World

"It takes a strong person to remain single in a world that is accustomed to settling with anything just to say I have something." – Anonymous

Society and culture make it seem like you have the black plague if you have decided to remain single and sexually abstinent. It is vital to wait on God, to reveal your mate to you. However, this world has made it extremely difficult to live a normal, healthy lifestyle as a Christian man or woman. If you are single and 30 years old or older, the world makes it seem like there is something wrong with you if you are not already happily married with children. Anywhere you settle your feet, nowadays, there are constant reminders that your "problem of singleness" can be quickly remedied. Just take a look at the top magazines at the grocery stores. So many of them broadcast relationship advice on the front cover, like the "5 Secrets of Finding Your Perfect Match" or "How to Meet the Perfect One Before the Holidays". Not to mention, your parents and married friends, are pressuring you to go on blind dates, because your parents want grandchildren and your friends just want you to be happy like them. The list can go on and on.

To add another layer of complexity, you may also have to deal with a few internal pressures as you get older. For example, if you want to have children, you may not be sure if your body will be able to handle having kids. Not to mention, the weight of your own insecurities holding you back because you are uncertain whether you are even capable of being a good parent, or if you are cut out to be a wife or a husband. When you are single in this modern world, it seems like you will never be able to get a break, until your wedding bells begin to ring. I know from experience that these are just common pressures that women face overall, but what about the men?

Men have their own issues that they fight with regarding singleness. Their pressures can range from needing to have enough money to care for a family, to trying to tackle what seems to be "the unattainable goal", that I believe has been placed on them, of not being able to commit to one woman for the rest of their lives. Once again, culture and society has put pressure on men, to find themselves by venturing out and dating as many women as they desire before settling down, because "there are many fish in the sea just waiting to be captured." Yuck! Not to mention, some men did not have the best role models growing up. They were either raised with an abusive and controlling father figure, or an emotionally absent father or they had no father figure at all. For some of these men, there was no one to teach them how to be an overall godly man and husband. In spite of these various upbringings, I believe all men are created in the wonderful image of God, and it takes a God-fearing man to realize that He is created in this perfect image. Therefore, as God's image bearers, these men also have the character of God, and that includes faithfulness; thus, making it possible for a man to commit to just one woman for the rest of their lives. I have met many men of God who are faithful husbands and many who are walking in purity while they are still single.

Though we all have our own gender-specific tensions, both women and men have the same struggles when it comes to the waiting process. It can be burdensome to trust that God knows what He is doing when it comes to the matters that deeply concerns your heart like waiting for marriage, waiting to have children, or waiting to be loved by that special someone. Whether you are a female or male reading this devotion, if you have the desire to be married, wait patiently for your Boaz or for your Rebekah to appear. Remember, it was the Lord who brought Ruth to Boaz's side (Ruth 3) and Rebekah to Isaac's field (Genesis 24). So be encouraged, and try not to worry about finding the right one, because Jesus will bring it all together in due time. ***Waiting is necessary.*** This is something you will probably have to tell yourself every time, when the wait does not seem worth it. During your waiting season with the Lord, you will learn how to love yourself, you will learn how you deserve to be loved, and the waiting period will better prepare you, on how to sacrificially love your future spouse and children the way Christ loves them.

<u>PRAYER:</u>

"Thank you, Father, for the grace you have given me to be single. Teach me the goodness there is in being single and teach me how to be the bride of Christ. Thank you, Lord, that you have the right person in mind for me. Keep my eyes focused on your will, your Word, and your ways, as I wait in this season. I pray for your peace to be in my heart. I know my steps are ordered in you. As I wait, I pray you will strengthen me to press towards the prize on heavenward in Christ. You have great plans for my life, and I choose to believe you will not pass me by. "Wonderful are your works in my life Lord and my soul knows them very well" (Psalm 139:14, ESV). In Jesus' name, I pray, Amen."

Devotion 23: Waiting for Your Boaz or Rebekah

"Dance with God until He lets someone cut in." – Anonymous

If you are single and you are waiting on God to be married, do yourself a favor, and take time to enjoy life. Your life does not begin when you get married. Marriage is just another chapter to your life. Live your life to the fullest and take much needed time to deepen your relationship with Jesus. ***Men and women of God there is a purpose to your singleness and it is meant to be fun.*** As long as God has promised you a mate, He will fulfill that which concerns your heart. Keep your trust in God, for He will bring the right one for you, at the right time. Waiting on the Lord to send the perfect spouse to you is one of the wisest decisions that you will ever make in your life. I use the term perfect loosely of course, because no one is perfect. However, because God chooses this person for you, he or she will be nothing short of perfection when it pertains to His divine will for you.

Subsequently, there are some people who think waiting on God for this special someone is pointless. They have their own list of credentials their future mate must match up to, and if they do not match up, then it is an automatic deal-breaker. Well, let me let you in on a little secret, it is all right to have a preference, but we should never allow our personal preferences to interfere with God's perfect plan for us.

The Discovery Process

The best place to find your significant other is in the presence of God. Just look at Isaac! In Genesis 24:63-64, Isaac was in the field in the evening time meditating on the Bible, when here comes Rebekah, coming not just into his town but also into his life, and eventually into his heart. This is a beautiful picture of how God can orchestrate the union of two people coming together, without either of them lifting a hand. All they needed to do, was to be in the right place at the right time. I do not agree with modern-day society, that tells us we need to date all these different types of people in order to find the "right one". God knows who He has for you. Isaac was in God's presence and God sent his wife to him. So, be encouraged man of God to sit still in God's presence, and as you are focusing on the Lord, one day you will look up, and your beautiful future wife will be coming to greet you.

In all honesty, women may possibly feel like they have a harder time waiting on the right man to appear, because the Bible says in Proverbs 18:22 (ESV), "He who finds a wife finds a good thing and obtains favor from the Lord". If you are a woman reading this, please do not think your life is centered around you being found by a man. Think of this verse as more of an encouragement. The man of God the Lord will send to you, he will see you as the good thing the Lord has blessed him with and you will add favor to his life. One day you will be found by the right man of God who understands you and who is graced to love you the way you deserve to be loved. You are a very special treasure to be sought after. If you have not been found yet, it is because God does not want you to marry, just any type of man. God desires for you to marry the man of God He has spiritually matured and chosen to be your husband. Just take a look at Ruth's life, in the book of Ruth chapters 1-3. Her previous husband dies, and she finds herself gleaning in Boaz's field and he pursued her. Without her knowing, Boaz was going to become her kinsman redeemer. You do not have to go searching for your husband, for the Lord will bring him to you or you to him, in due time. Continue to stay focused and remain faithful to what God is asking you to do in this present time.

Finally, to both my brothers and sisters out there, *remember singleness is not a punishment.* It is a time to enjoy who God has made you to be. It is a time of freedom. So be encouraged, to have fun with your friends and have fun being the awesome person you are. Work on bettering yourself. Do not be concerned with someone having to come into your life to make you a better you, to make you feel complete, or to make you feel like you are finally experiencing life. Only God can do that. Your life is found in God and there is so much for you to fulfill while you are single. For some of you, God is calling you to be successful in writing books, doing missions, building a business, preaching the gospel, and overall, advancing the kingdom of God in your singleness. Before you know it, you will end up exactly where you need to be, and your spouse from the Lord will be waiting for you. God will send your ordained, perfected in Christ, God-fearing, spouse to you. *People of God, waiting is not easy but when God's plan begins to come to pass in your life, you will see that this powerhouse that God is about to join together, has been worth the wait after all.*

<u>PRAYER:</u>

"Dear Father God, my prayer is that I will become solely content in you. Please help me get to a place where, I am completely satisfied to fulfill your purpose for me in my singleness. Lord I pray that you will, redirect my heart's passions, drives, and desires, to be focused on living my best single life now with you Jesus. Like Solomon says in the book of Song of Solomon 8:4 (NIV & NLT), help me to "not arouse or awaken love until it so desires" or "awaken love until the time is right." Lord you make everything beautiful in its' time. I want your best for me, Lord: the best spouse, the best mate, the best friend who will stick by me, and the best person who you have chosen for me to have children with. I choose to wait for you Lord, and for the one you have for me. You are both worth waiting for. In Jesus' name, I pray, Amen."

Devotion 24: Your Life is Blessed

(The Life of Rachel Part 1)

It is only with gratitude that life becomes rich. –
Dietrich Bonhoeffer

Life is full of surprises. There are some surprises that will make you smile with inexpressible joy, and then there are those surprises, where you get some devastating news, that will change your life forever. You may be wondering, "Is this really happening to me?" Or yet, you may be asking yourself and God, "Why is this happening to me?" Life has a sense of humor of its own that is not always funny. Let us just be real, life can be unfair at times. It will not always play out the way you want it to or even end up the way you have prayed for. So, when life gives you lemons, you have to be willing to buy some sugar, take out your stirring stick, and get a glass of ice water to make yourself some good-ole fashioned lemonade. When bad news comes your way, you can either choose to stay mad or choose to rest in the Lord. The experiences you have in this life are truly what you decide to make of them.

Paul encourages us in James 1:2-4 (AMP) to, "Consider it pure joy my brothers and sisters, whenever you fall into various trials. Be assured that the testing of your faith [through experience] produces steadfastness and endurance [leading to spiritual maturity, and inner peace]. And let endurance have its perfect result and do thorough work, so that you may be perfect and completely developed [in your faith], lacking nothing." Be of good cheer in knowing that although trials will come, most assuredly they will not last forever. They are here to make you stronger and wiser. The long-lasting work God is doing in you will equip you to withstand all sorts of adversity. Just continue to put your faith in Christ, and you will triumph over every trial that comes your way.

The work God is performing in your life reminds me of what He was doing in Rachel's life in Genesis chapter 30. God was doing something good in Rachel's life, but it was hard for her to see the evidence of His goodness because of her barrenness. God was looking to bless Rachel, but she needed to know that she was blessed regardless of her situation. Seeing that her life was not going exactly how she had planned, possibly discouraged her faith in God. I believe Rachel's inability to have children could have made her feel like she was not blessed by God. In the Jewish culture, when a woman could not have children, they were viewed as being cursed. Like-wise, your life experiences may have helped you draw the same conclusion about yourself; that you are not blessed because you are barren in some area of your life. Life has hit you with countless gut-wrenching situations. For instance, you probably did not get into your dream school or get your dream job. You could have had a miscarriage, lost a loved one in a car accident, or you have been fired from your job. Perhaps, you cannot find the right mate, your significant other left you or cheated on you, or you cannot break an addiction. Maybe you are sad because you have no true friends, or you have been diagnosed with a terminal illness.

Whatever is happening in your life right now, you may feel like God is not with you. Rachel probably felt the same way. First, her sister steals her husband right from under her nose and then her sister is bearing all of his children. Surprisingly enough, if you take time to read the rest of the story, you will find that Rachel's real problem was not with Leah and it was not with Jacob. It was with God. Same can be true with you. Some of you have held grudges in your heart towards God because of the bad things that have happened to you or to your loved ones. I can totally relate to this because, there was a time I was seriously angry with God, because I thought He took my mother home to heaven prematurely. After going to counseling and after many tearful nights in prayer, I watched, as God ministered His peace to my heart. Eventually, I was able to release my anger into His hands and now I have peace. I believe in our seasons of brokenness God will show us how much He loves us, and He will prove to us that we are His blessed children.

We cannot continue to believe that every impossible situation that stands before us, is life's way of letting us know that we are cursed. ***It is not the tangible things that we have or the things that we are waiting for, that determines whether or not we are blessed. We are blessed because we know God, we are blessed because we belong to God, and we are blessed because God belongs to us.***

So be encouraged, for I believe God is here and He is going to change your situation around. God is going to give you insight on how to deal with your current problems. I pray that God gives you a fresh new pair of lenses, to see your life through the eyes of the Savior and not from a place of brokenness. When you are quiet and reflective in His presence, you will realize the good things, God has prepared for you, they will far outweigh the tribulations of life. As the Psalmist says, "Be still and know that He is God" (Psalm 46:10 NIV). He will not let your enemies that have come to wear you down, overtake you. When life throws stones at you to crush you, God will enable you to catch each one, to keep them as a memorial to remember His faithfulness. God will then teach you, how to take these stones to build an altar of praise, to exalt Him above what you are going through; for He holds your life in the palm of His hands.

<u>PRAYER:</u>

"Father, I pray that my confidence will forever be in you. You are the author of my life and I surrender my life into your hands. My life is best when lived in and through you Jesus. Help me to know that I am blessed and teach me how to walk in your blessings for me. I pray that you will heal my heart from impatience and anger towards you and others Lord. I declare I am blessed and cannot be cursed, in Jesus' name. Father help me to believe that you have not forgotten me. Thank you, Father, for the patience to wait for the blessings you have for me, and for the courage to wait on you every day. Your timing is perfect, and your ways are beyond my understanding. I choose to serve and magnify you, Lord, and not my problems and trials. In Jesus' name, Amen."

Devotion 25: God is Bigger Than Your *Not Yet* Blessing

(The Life of Rachel Part 2)

When Rachel saw that she conceived no children for Jacob, she envied [was jealous of] her sister, and she said to Jacob, "Give me children, or else I will die." Then Jacob become furious with Rachel, and he said, "Am I in the place of God, who has denied you children?" – Genesis 30:1-2 (AMP)

What do you do, when you feel like, you should have a particular blessing already, but it is not here yet? You may be questioning the situation and asking yourself, "Is God not ready to bless me?" or "Am I not ready to receive it?" Either way, being denied something that you are genuinely desperate for, can leave you in anguish. Rachel in Genesis chapter 30, as mentioned in the previous devotion, was denied the ability to have children and she did not know why. This left her bitter and angry. Have you ever been so frustrated with life, that you took out your anger on everyone around you? Your anger seeps through your attitude and conversations to the point, people are scared to approach you. Although you may be justified in being angry because your situations are unfair, I would encourage you, to not allow your anger to consume you. **When we focus too much**

on what we do not have, we will mess up the things we do have: the blessings that are right in front of us.

I would recommend for you to re-read this Bible story, and as you do you will find that Rachel lacked confidence in God, as some of us do. Because of this, she took her frustrations out on Jacob and Leah. First, she blamed her husband Jacob for not giving her children, and then she was envious of her sister Leah because she was fertile, and Rachel was not. Rachel looked to these two as her source of healing and as her problem solvers, when the reality was, only God held the key to fixing her problem. God was the only one who could open her womb. I do not personally know what you are facing at this moment, but I know whatever it is, only God is able to get you out. The people in your life, no matter what role they play or the influence they have over you, they do not have the power to make your life better; only God can do that. I believe He is going to turn your situation around today.

In Genesis 30:22 (AMP) the Bible says, "Then God remembered [the prayers of] Rachel, and God thought of her and opened her womb [so that she could conceive]". God alone was able to get to the root of Rachel's problem by healing her womb and her heart. Rachel's issue was not nearly as big as her God. Rachel rejoiced in the Lord after she gave birth to her son Joseph and in Genesis 30:23 (AMP) she said, "God has taken away my disgrace and humiliation". Your issues are no match for your Almighty God. When God gave Rachel her blessing, He gave her a double portion of two children: Joseph and Benjamin, therefore, exceeding her prayer requests. Rachel wanted just one baby, whereas God wanted to give her more than she could even imagine. Her first child Joseph was the Old Testament depiction of the soon coming Savior Jesus Christ. In addition, Joseph played a major role in the nation of Israel's history by helping Israel and Egypt survive a severe famine. ***God was not looking to purely bless her with an ordinary blessing, but with an extraordinary blessing. He is getting ready to do the same thing*** *for you. The blessings that the Lord has for you are going to make you rich, happy, and will far exceed your heart's desires.*

What are you asking your heavenly Father for today? You may be asking God for a house when He wants to give you a mansion so that you can also house the homeless. You may be asking God for a new car and He wants to bless you with an entire car dealership, so that you can be a blessing to single mothers in your city. You may be asking God for a promotion on your job and He wants to bless you with your own business. You may be sick in your body, and you are asking God to take away the pain for a little while. When in fact, God wants to heal you entirely, so that you can testify to the nations that your God still heals. Do not limit what God is able to do for you and through you. The blessings that God is about to give to you for His purpose, will leave you in awe of His glorious power.

So be encouraged, and instead of thinking of your situations as "problems", try to think of them as opportunities and places where God is able to supernaturally intervene. When we have this mindset, we make space for God to perform miracles in our impossibilities. Be encouraged to trust in God again and to rejoice when others are blessed. Know that your *on-time-double-blessing* is surely on its' way. Just believe it and you shall receive it!

<u>PRAYER:</u>

"Father my soul rejoices when I think of all your goodness towards me. Help me to always remember all the great things that you have done, fulfilled, and accomplished in my life so far. I want to have a heart full of thankfulness and gratitude towards the wonderful things you have done for me. Help me to rejoice with those whom you have blessed. Help me to not be bitter and angry when I see them being blessed. Give me your joy. Teach me to trust in your Word and to know that you are blessing me. I will not allow jealousy and anger to take a bitter root in my heart anymore. I declare, my heart is filled with God's love for others and for myself. I am secure within His presence. I am appreciative of what you have given me, and I know that you have not abandoned me. I will get my blessings in due time; God's time. I command my heart to wait and to trust in God, so that I can learn to enjoy life in and with you, Lord. I am already blessed, for you are my blessing, Father. I love you. In Jesus' name, I pray, Amen."

Devotion 26: Trusting God

(The Life of Rachel Part 3)

"He has made everything beautiful in its time. He has also set eternity in the human heart; yet no one can fathom what God has done from beginning to end." - Ecclesiastes 3:1 (NIV)

God makes everything beautiful in His time and He has the perfect plan set out for your life. Every single step is ordered and set in place for you to walk into it. God knows what is going to work for you and He knows what is not going to work. He knows what is going to make you happy for eternity and He knows the things that will make you miserable for a lifetime. Since you and I both know that God is omniscient, He loves us, and He will never hurt us, then why is it so hard for us to trust that He has the best plan for us? I think the answer comes down to three factors: we are very impatient, fearful, and worrisome about God's timing. You may be wondering, "Is God going to bless me?" "When is God going to bless me?" And, "How is God going to bless me?" Your fear will lead you to doubt God and doubt His plan for your life. Pastor Rick Warren puts it like this:

> "God encourages His followers to 'fear not' 365 times in the Bible, one for each day of the year. God did not intend for Christians to spend their

days preoccupied with anxiety and worry. When Christians form a healthy relationship with God and understand His eternal grace and mercy, they realize that there is no real need for fear."

The truth is, God is going to bless you. He has a great track record on fulfilling His promises concerning your life. The question is not, "Will God do it for you?", the question is, "Will you trust God to be God in your life to do it for you?"

For some of you, God has already given you a few things on your checklist. But, there are just a couple of more things that have not happened for you yet. You have been longing for these blessings and it feels like you have been waiting for an eternity to receive what has been promised to you. Even though I know you do not want to hear this, there is a reason why your blessing is not here yet.

Like I mentioned in the two previous devotions, Rachel the wife of Jacob, knew all about the hardships of trusting in God. While she was learning how to trust God, she had to watch while God was blessing her sister and possibly the other women around her with children. The same goes for you. You may be watching while all your friends and family members are being blessed with marriage, having children, running successful businesses, graduating from top universities, getting the best jobs, driving the latest cars, wearing fashionable clothes, and living in the most expensive houses, while you are still having to patiently wait on the Lord to bless you.

Your journey with the Lord is special, personal, and intimate; it is not worth comparing. The path God is choosing to take you on is designed specifically for you. When it comes down to it, God is making a name for Himself in your life. So, do not waste your time coveting what others have. Even if you cannot see it right now, God is working on your behalf, and it is far better than anything you can even imagine. God is building your trust for Him. If you learn to build your trust muscles in the Lord, you will see He has the best in mind for you. Some of you reading this right now, may not like where you are, and you may be questioning where you are going, but like this anonymous saying states, "Difficult roads often lead to beautiful destinations." Once arriving at this beautiful destination, I believe you will rejoice and thank God for taking His time with you.

So, stop rushing God to bless you, because you may just get what you have been asking for, and it may not be all, you thought it would be. *Your Father knows what He is doing. The blessings God has for you are not premature or delayed, but they will always come on time.* Do your best to not give up waiting on the Lord. For Rachel, there was a point in time where she gave up waiting on God to bless her with a child. She took matters into her own hands by allowing her servant to lay with her husband. I believe she did not wait on God because she had trust issues, like some of us do. Could it be that God is waiting for you to take your hands off of the steering wheel of your life before He intervenes? God does not need your help to move your life forward. He does not need your plan B or suggestions on how to get things going because His plan A is under control. You do not have to force yourself to be blessed or to attain God's blessings. You will always be blessed because you are a child of God. I believe God's blessings will always draw us closer to Him and not from Him. God wants us to be happy in the promises He has for us, but He would not have us compromise our moral integrity in order to be blessed. God's blessings make us rich and He adds no sorrow with it (Proverbs 10:22 ESV).

So be encouraged, for those of you who are feeling disappointed, while waiting on the Lord. I would challenge you to stir up your faith, by trying to remember the last time God came through for you on His Word. The same God who did it for you back then is the same God right now. So, what do you do in this awkward place of waiting for your *not yet* blessing? Well, you do your best to trust God. Keep persevering, stay focused on your Jesus-centered goals, and keep believing that your prayers are leaving an imprint in your Savior's heart.

<u>PRAYER:</u>

"Father God, teach me how to trust and how to wait on you. My heart is heavy in waiting on your promises for my life. I release all of my frustrations, fear, and worries to you. I command my heart to bless the Lord and to wait patiently on you. Jesus, deal with the issues of my heart. You have the best blessings in store for me. All things are working out for my good because I am a beloved child of God. Father your plans for me are way better than the ones I have for myself. Help me to stay focused on what is required of me right now. Help me to not rely on my own methods, to bless myself. Please remove all distractions from my life. Help me to not covet others' blessings. I pray that the blessings that I have, or the ones I am waiting for, will never become an idol in my life. You are a Promise Keeper, the lifter of my head, the source of my strength, and I declare my soul will trust in you, Lord. In Jesus's name, I pray, Amen."

PART 4.

Fighting A Victorious Battle:

Spiritual Warfare

Devotion 27: You Have Authority

"You were dead because of your sins and because your sinful nature was not yet cut away. Then God made you alive with Christ, for he forgave all our sins. He canceled the record of the charges against us and took it away by nailing it to the cross. In this way, he disarmed the spiritual rulers and authorities. He shamed them publicly by his victory over them on the cross." - Colossians 2 verses 13-15 (NLT)

Jesus is the superhero for all Christians, the undefeated champion of heaven and earth. If you are into comics or movies, you know that every superhero has a wicked villain who has it out for him or her. For Jesus and for Christians, our wicked villain and enemy is the devil. He also goes by the name of Satan or the accuser of the brethren. All day and night the devil tries to accuse God's people of wrongdoing. We never have to worry about the bad image he tries to paint in God's mind about us, because God knows he is a liar. The enemy has no charge to hold against us because through the blood of Jesus, we are found not guilty. This is such an awesome grace, wonderful love, and glorious freedom that has been given to us.

The basic rundown is that the devil has had it out for you before you were even born. Now that you are on this earth desiring to serve the Lord, He is going to try every trick in his book to get you to fail. Guess again, devil. The Bible says in Isaiah 54:17 (NKJV), "No weapon formed against you shall prosper." That means every hidden scheme, ALL devices, and ALL plots the enemy has set up for you to fall into, in order to kill you, will not work. "Why?" Because of the blood of Jesus. Jesus told the devil on the cross, "You cannot have this one!" "I have died for my child, and my child belongs to me." ***The same authority Jesus has over the enemy, He has given to you.*** In Luke 10:19 (NIV), Jesus said, "I have given you authority to trample over snakes and scorpions and to overcome ALL the power of the enemy; nothing will harm you." Jesus has now put the ball in your court and how you exercise this authority is up to you.

Daily meditation, memorization, recitation, and prophetic declaration of the Word of God, will prepare you for any fight against the devil. God's Word will forever disarm the devil's lies from having any place in your life. In 1 Peter 5:8 (NIV), the Bible says, "Be alert and of sober mind. Your enemy, the devil, prowls around like a roaring lion looking for someone to devour." Basically, he is all bark and no bite. So, do not give him anything to latch onto or to sink his teeth into. The devil is like a bully at school, who taunts the little wimpy kid for weeks until the wimpy kid steps up to the plate and gets his older sibling to kick that bully's butt. Typically, after getting beaten up, the bully runs away because deep inside he is a coward. This is the depiction of the enemy. He is the real coward. He prowls around you, throwing negative words at you in hopes of discouraging you. All the devil has is words: negative, defiled, annoying, rude and crude words. If he can get these words to influence your soul, heart, and mind, he will have a hold on you. The enemy will try to get you to focus on his lies, instead of focusing on God's truth.

There is a clear depiction of this in Genesis chapter 3. When the serpent (the devil) approached Eve, he tried to get her to question the voice of God; "Did God really say that?" And then Eve did what you and I tend to do; we meditate on what the enemy is saying, instead of automatically rebuking it. Eve allowed doubt to seep in, and sometimes we do the same thing, we open the door for doubt and confusion to come in. Eve opened the gates of her heart, soul, and mind to be deceived. When we open our gates to be deceived, that becomes the entrance way for the enemy to begin stealing and robbing us of our peace and joy. The enemy will do everything he can to try to prohibit us from accomplishing our purpose in God. Today, it is time for you and I to be like that wimpy kid, by stepping up to the devil to tell him, "You cannot bully me around anymore! I serve a God who is greater than you, and my God is coming to strike you down devil!"

Jesus is giving you success on every side. According to Colossians 2:13 (NIV), Jesus has already shamed the enemy publicly on your behalf. So, take your stand and declare that the enemy can no longer try to impose shame on you privately, with deceptive and perverted thoughts that he throws at you, in your bedroom in the midnight hours. The next time the enemy comes to you with his negative words, do not retaliate with your own words. Jesus in Matthew chapter 4, has given you one of the greatest keys to the kingdom. He has handed you the biggest weapon of ALL: The Word of God. The Word of God will build up your identity and your confidence in Christ. Declare the Word of God and the devil will flee.

The Word of God is strong and powerful. When you use it to combat the enemy, it puts him in his rightful place, which is directly under your feet. You are amplifying the works of the cross when you speak the Word back at the enemy. You are stating that you attest and have faith in what Jesus has done for you and you are declaring that Jesus is greater than that wicked serpent. In the Garden of Eden, Adam and Eve gave the devil their authority, by disobeying God. Jesus came and reversed things back to their original order and gave us back our authority through His blood. Where Adam failed, Jesus prevailed! Jesus took away Satan's power to torment you, to bother you, and to continuously prick thorns at your heart. The enemy is rendered powerless before you.

So be encouraged, to take your weapons of warfare, which are of divine power, and demolish and destroy the works of the enemy. God is changing the way you fight and He is transforming your mind, to see yourself as a conquering warrior. You will no longer have to fight for your victory. Now, you can fight from a place of victory. Take up your position as a child of the living King, standing firm and wearing the Word of God as your garment of warfare. If you continue to know who you are in Christ, you will be a force to be reckoned with.

PRAYER:

"Jesus, help me to take back the authority that you have given me on this earth. Help me to daily demobilize the enemy with your Word the way that you have disarmed him from having authority, jurisdiction, and power in my life. I break every generational curse over me in Jesus' name, and I no longer allow the devil to reign over my family and over my life, in Jesus' name. I take everything that you have for me by force. I believe the Lord Almighty is fighting my every battle. I am strong in the Lord and in the power of His might. I believe that there is more for me than that which is against me. I am not defeated. I am an overcomer. I am more than a conqueror and I have already won through the blood of Jesus Christ, which strengthens me. Thank you, Jesus, for strengthening me and for quickening my feet to be sustained in you, Lord. In Jesus' name, I pray, Amen."

Devotion 28: Don't Look Back

"But one thing I do: Forgetting what lies behind and reaching forward to what lies ahead."- Philippians 3:12 (AMP)

When you are constantly looking back at how things used to be, you will miss out on what is to come. When you are too past-conscious instead of being completely present-focused and future driven, it can cause you severe consequences. You can inevitably miss out on God's divine purpose and promises for your life, because you are waiting and hoping for the past to repeat itself. ***If the past was meant to repeat itself then it would have made it into your future, and since it did not, it is time to let it go.*** You need to learn how to forget the former things of old because God has many newer and greater blessings to give to you. The Bible says in Isaiah 43:18-20, before God gives you these new blessings, He announces and reveals them to you. When you place your trust in the Lord, you can look forward to having a hopeful future in Him. Your present days will be way brighter than the dark clouds of your past.

In Genesis chapter 19, the Bible teaches us the importance of letting go of the past. In this chapter we read about Lot's wife, who took one last glimpse at her past and this cost Lot's wife, her life. She lived in Sodom with her family, which was formerly known as one of the most wicked cities in the world. The Lord sent angels to warn

Sodom and Gomorrah of their rebellion and sins, but they chose not to turn from their evil ways. So, the Lord sent fire to destroy the cities. But on behalf of Abraham, God spared Lot and his wife. On the day of judgment, when her entire family was running away towards safety, Lot's wife turned around to take one more look at the place she once called home. She probably also got distracted by the screams of the people that were being judged. These were the same people that tried to harm her husband and were willing to harm her daughters. Lot's wife was more focused on the terror that was behind her than the victory that was in front of her. ***Do not become distracted by your past. It is a dangerous thing that can rob you of getting to your place of destiny.***

God has come to deliver you from your past. The enemy, on-the-other-hand, is a liar and he will try his best to make you feel condemned and stuck in your past. Some of the ways he will try to keep you bound include: putting vulgar images in your mind or bringing people back into your life who are not good for you, in order to make you stagnate and non-progressive. For some of you, completely letting go of the past, especially a former relationship, is a hard thing to do. When sin comes knocking at your door, the enticement from it is compelling, alluring and sometimes hard to resist. Paul says in Romans 7 verses 15 and 17 (ESV), "For I do not understand my own actions. For I do not do what I want, but I do the very thing I hate. So now it is no longer I who do it, but sin that dwells within me." It is as if you are bounded to the sins that are dwelling deep within you or you are soul-tied to the sins of your past. When you are at a point of weakness or having a tough time in your life, or better yet, when everything seems to be going just right, that is when the past comes knocking at your door. It can come in the form of past lovers or bad friendships, or addictions such as: pornography, masturbation, smoking, sex, and drinking. These things will creep up out of nowhere, trying to invade your life again.

Even for some of you, right now, the temptation to look back is so much stronger than your will-power to move forward and to overcome the burden of sin. Like Oswald Chambers says, we have to learn to "leave the broken, irreversible past in God's hands, and step out into the invincible future with Him." When God tells you to leave certain people or things in the past, you are no longer responsible for them. God has given you the capacity and the ability to leave those things behind you forever. When you take time to really think about it, you do not need something or someone in your life, that God does not even see as, beneficial enough to make it into your future.

Getting completely away from your past, cannot be done by your own willpower, but with Jesus' power that lives in you. Rely on God's grace for you, then you will be able to slam the door in the face of your past, declaring, "No more!" and "Enough is enough!" There are other profitable steps you are going to have to take as well. You are going to have to filter what you watch on television, at the movies, and on your computer. You will have to leave certain friends behind and delete certain phone numbers from your cell phone. You will have to actively take back your life by giving up certain habits; like putting that bottle, needle, and cigarette down for the last time. You will have to walk away from that particular guy or lady friend that you have been having premarital sex or committing adultery with. **Basically, you will have to leave the past right where it is, so it can stop holding you back.** It is time for you to be fully restored and healed. Other measures you will have to take include memorizing and reciting Scriptures over your life, speaking in tongues daily, praying in the Spirit, fasting, seeking professional and spiritual help and getting a prayer partner to agree with you. You will have to make whatever sacrifices necessary to remove anything that will attract you back to that sin that so easily entangles and binds you.

For some of you, you will have to endure fighting a daily battle. Praise Jesus, you will never have to fight alone. The best way to stay victorious is to spend much time in the presence of God through worship, praise, and reading of the Word. As you do this, the Lord will reveal to you the origination of where these sins came from. As well as, He will show you what demonic influences are tempting you, so that you can rebuke these demons from your life in Jesus' name. Most of your habits and addictions have stemmed from a lie that you have believed in childhood, resulting from a childhood trauma, or feelings of loneliness or abandonment. I attended a seminar last year called Blessing Generations* with Pastor Craig Hill. It really changed my life because God showed me what my emotional triggers were, that kept leading me back into sin. During the seminar, I was able to hear God's voice and God's truth about how He sees me. God spoke to me and let me know that He was always there with me during my childhood when my father walked away. After confronting the past and expelling the deception of the devil's lies from my heart, I received God's love for me, and since then, I have been triumphant over these temptations. So be encouraged, for one day, you too will walk triumphantly in all God has called you to be.

When you finally decide to let go of your past, something better will always come along. Have the courage to let go of the old days and embrace the new days the Lord has made for you. You cannot move forward if you are still holding on to what could have been. Like this anonymous quote says, "It hurts to let go, but sometimes it hurts *(you)* more to hold on."

*If you are interested in partaking in a Blessing Generations Seminar, please check out this website. It is truly life-changing.
https://craighill.org/blessing-generations/

<u>PRAYER:</u>

"Father, thank you for giving me strength for the battles I have to fight. Thank you for giving me the victory for the battles I have seen, and for the ones that are still unknown to me. Thank you for your warring angels, even now, that encamp around me (Psalm 34:7). I pray the fear of the Lord will cause dread to fall upon the heads of my enemies. Help me to forget my past and to move forward from it. Help me to make wise decisions as I move forward in you. The battle is yours, God. Victory has always belonged to Jesus, and victory is now mine. I place my will, my past, my pride, and my understanding of spiritual warfare into your hands. Lord, train my hands for battle, my fingers for war, and my mind to stay on you. I pray Ephesians chapter 6:11-17 (ESV) over my life:

"*I* put on the whole armor of God, that *I* may be able to stand against the schemes of the devil. For *I* do not wrestle against flesh and blood, but against the rulers, against the authorities, against the cosmic powers over this present darkness, against the spiritual forces of evil in the heavenly places. Therefore, *I* take up the whole armor of God, that *I* may be able to withstand in the evil day, and having done all, to stand firm. Stand therefore, having fastened on the belt of truth, and having put on the breastplate of righteousness, and as shoes for *my* feet, having put on the readiness given by the gospel of peace. In all circumstances *I* take up the shield of faith, with which *I* can extinguish all the flaming darts, *accusations, and weapons* of the evil one; and take the helmet of salvation, and the sword of the Spirit, which is the word of God."

"With your Word Lord I will destroy all wickedness over my life and I will discern your truth. I surrender my will, this battle, my life, my all, and my family to you. In Jesus' name, Amen."

Devotion 29: Get Back Your Stolen Goods

"In the midst of the storm, don't be impressed with the amount of rainfall or the wind or waves beating on your life. But be more impressed with the One who is walking on the water, silencing the wind and rebuking the waves. The One who bids you to come and meet Him. He the most Impressive of them all." – Laurine Voltaire

"The storm will be over soon", "This too shall pass", or "This is just a season", are comforting phrases we typically hear, or even say to ourselves, when we are going through some crazy times. Though they are very true, and although things do get better after a while, the storms in our lives typically get worse before they get better. Right now, you may be feeling as if you are stuck on a ship in the most chaotic storm ever, and you are being pushed on every side. This storm is messing with your blessings: your family, your job, your finances, your health, your emotions, and basically everything you love and care about. You are overwhelmed, and the cares of life are flooding your heart to the point where you feel like you are drowning in the sea of despair. It is harder than ever to believe that God will see you through to the other side. Today, I have good news for you. Jesus is on His way and He is coming to speak to your storm. And the promises the enemy is trying to take away from you have not been damaged, torn, decreased, depleted or used up. They are STILL GOOD. God gives good gifts to His children and He has given you the authority to rebuke the enemy from stealing your gifts.

When you look at the lives of the Israelites in the Old Testament, you will see that they were faced with all sorts of adversity in their journey from Egypt to the wilderness, and while they were trying to make it to the Promised Land. Before getting to the Promised Land, the Israelites had to defeat multiple enemies including: the Hittites, Amorites, Canaanites, Perizzites, Hivites, and Jebusites (Deuteronomy 20:17). I can imagine the devil trying to steal their joy during the journey, by injecting fear into their hearts, because of the size of their enemies. *In what areas of your life, has the enemy tried to rob you of your joy and confidence in God? The enemy will try to make you think that, these situations that stand before you are greater than your living God.* But know this, that even when the devil comes to steal, kill, and destroy your life, Jesus has come to give you life and life more abundantly (John 14:6). Today, you have to declare, you will no longer allow the devil to prevent you from making it to your Promised Land.

There is an appointed time when you will see victory in every area of your life, guaranteed. This appointed time is called PAYDAY. *Payday is the day when God demands the devil to give you back everything he has stolen.* Through prophetic warfare, intercessions, declarations, and praise and worship, you will go into the enemy's camp to take back all he has taken from you....AND THEN SOME. The enemy thought he could count you out of this race. Guess again, devil! Through Jesus Christ and through the power of the blood, I declare, the devil has lost again.

I am believing that you will receive double for your trouble. This is the season where the Lord will make your enemies at peace with you. Our God is a God of increase, and the struggle and turmoil you have gone through will not be overlooked. He is Yahweh Gemûlāh: The

God of RECOMPENSE. He is also the God of VINDICATION, RETALIATION, RESTITUTION, and REPAY.

It is about time that you come out of this storm. When you do, you will come out looking and smelling better than when you went in. Just ask Shadrach, Meshach, and Abednego, as seen in Daniel chapter 3. Jesus met them in the fire, as He is meeting you in your storm, and He brought them out, with not even a hint of smoke on their clothing. It may feel like you have been in the fire for such a long time, and it seems like it is getting even hotter now, in this season of your life. But just continue to hold on. God's promise to us is that when we walk through the fire, we will not be burned, and we will not be set ablaze. His presence will always be there with us (Isaiah 43:2).

So be encouraged, for I see a fresh wind from heaven coming your way and it is going to turn your storms in another direction. God is fighting for you. What the locust have eaten and what the cankerworm has destroyed, the Lord will restore. God is lifting up a standard against all your enemies. They will come in one direction and they will flee in seven and you will watch with your eyes and see the deliverance of the Lord. By faith, you will see a hundred-fold of blessings being returned to you and you will receive your well-deserved harvest in no time.

<u>PRAYER:</u>

"Thank you, Lord, that you are going to restore all that the enemy has stolen. I declare a full return in my life, in Jesus' name. I do not have to be afraid or fearful, for you have redeemed me from captivity. You have called me by name and I am yours. When I pass through the fire Lord, you will be with me. As I walk through the rivers, they will not overwhelm me because you are there. When I walk through the fire, I will go untouched. I will not be scorched, and the flame will not burn me. For you are the Lord my God, the Holy One of Israel, my Savior, and you have given my enemies as my ransom because I am precious in your sight (Isaiah 43:1-4 AMP). Thank you for repaying to me everything that I have lost over the years. Help me to trust this process and help me to see the light at the end of the tunnel. Although I am walking through the darkest valley of my life, you are there with me, so there is Light in this day. I am assured you will sustain me and keep me strengthened in thy glorious grace. Jesus, thank you that my best days are coming. And thank you for the storehouse of blessings that are being returned to me because of your great faithfulness and your tender mercies towards me. In Jesus' name, I pray, Amen."

Devotion 30: You Always Win: Power Over a Defeated Foe

"The enemy is not fighting you because you are weak, he is fighting you because you are strong and you have a purpose." - Anonymous

Have you ever felt discouraged, or defeated, like your world was coming to an end? Even right now, you may be feeling like the ground you are walking on is crumbling right underneath you. Life is hitting you with wave after wave of disappointment and you do not know what to do. The enemy is trying to break you down and take you out. His constant harassment can cause you to fall into a severe depression, and it can even make you become suicidal. The real agenda of the enemy is to get into your head to play his endless mind games. He wants you to think that God is against you when He really is for you. The devil also wants you to feel like there is no way out of these situations and hardships. He would love it more than anything for you to die in your circumstance and to let it get the best of you. ***BUT YOU ARE NOT DEFEATED!*** You shall live and not die and declare the works of the Lord (Psalm 118:17). The power of the blood of Jesus gives you total victory, and once you realize this, there will be no stopping you. The fact that you are still alive to tell your story and the fact that this thing (problem, issue, diagnosis, divorce, sickness, job loss, loss of a relative, whatever it is) that should have killed you could not, shows that the devil's plans will never prosper. He is the defeated one and you are more than victorious.

God has given you the ability to change your circumstances by your faith and with the power of your tongue. So, whatever is standing before you today, rebuke it with your tongue, in Jesus' name. It might seem like a great mountain, but it is only the size of a pebble before your living God. Get ready to kick all the devil is trying to throw your way into the heart of the sea, where it can drown and torment you no more. For God has given you power over a defeated foe.

Did you know, that you are fighting against a devil that has already received his eternal punishment to burn forever? This means that you are combatting a defeated foe that has no legal ties or rights to you, unless you give it to him through willfully engaging in sin. Jesus defeated the enemy on the cross and He no longer has any authority over you. Therefore, through Jesus' blood, crucifixion, death, resurrection, and ascension, you have the power to defeat anything and everything that comes against you.

You have nothing in common with the enemy. You win, and he loses. You get to rejoice and go to heaven, and he gets to burn in hell. So, do not allow him to intimidate you. Do not make space in your life for him to come in and out as he pleases, to cause chaos and confusion. The devil lost that right once you gave your life to Jesus Christ. When you trust God with your life and all that entails: the good, the bad, the ugly and the beautiful, God will make sure that He works out everything for His good pleasure and for your good. What God has declared and made good in your life; the devil cannot curse. And the devil cannot try to steal away from you anything that has been rightfully given to you as an inheritance for being a child of God.

So be encouraged, and declare, that you have a mind of freedom and peace, and complete unity with the Father. Leave the defeated one in Jesus' hands. Take your life back and start walking with your head held up high towards the sky. It is time for you to start living your best life fully encouraged in the Lord. So, wave goodbye to your worries, wave goodbye to the devil, and wave goodbye to all the things that used to get you down. And today say hello to the new you, who is not bothered by the devil's schemes, the new you who walks victoriously as a child of God, and the new you who is destined to win. Now, let me hear you say it out loud and proud, *"I AM A WINNER!"*

<u>PRAYER:</u>

"Father, I cast my cares on you. I know I can depend on your goodness towards me, and I know that I do not have to fear anything or any bad news. All my life, my family, and all that concerns me is in your hands. Help me to stand in my authority against the enemy, so I will not fall into his mind games. I plead the blood of Jesus and I cover my thoughts and my emotions in the name of Jesus. I declare I will make it. I rebuke the devil from my life in the name of Jesus. I declare every door that has been opened to him is now shut in Jesus' name. Jesus, you are my safeguard and protection from all the devices of the enemy. I will be successful, and everything around me and concerning me is blessed. I am seated in heavenly places with Jesus. I am called to walk in victory. I am standing on you, Christ Jesus, my solid rock. In Jesus' name, I pray, Amen."

Printed in the United States
By Bookmasters